08/11

As one of ...

Thom...

guidebooks ... of destinations around the ...
sharing with travellers a wealth of

t...

Missing Pages

CUNARD

THE MOST FAMOUS OCEAN LINERS IN THE WORLD™

24 Hour Loan Only

Library Services by Ocean Books
www.oceanbooks.com

guides

CE

lton

6018

Written by Susie Boulton, updated by Jo-Ann Titmarsh
Original photography by Dario Mitidieri

Published by Thomas Cook Publishing
A division of Thomas Cook Tour Operations Limited
Company registration no. 3772199 England
The Thomas Cook Business Park, Unit 9, Coningsby Road,
Peterborough PE3 8SB, United Kingdom
Email: books@thomascook.com, Tel: +44 (0) 1733 416477
www.thomascookpublishing.com

Produced by Cambridge Publishing Management Limited
Burr Elm Court, Main Street, Caldecote CB23 7NU
www.cambridgepm.co.uk

ISBN: 978-1-84848-429-0

Series Editor: Karen Beaulah
Production/DTP: Steven Collins

Printed and bound in Spain by GraphyCems

Cover photography © Luca Da Ros/SIME/4Corners

Contents

Background 4–19
Introduction 4
The city 6
History 8
Politics 12
Culture 14
Festivals 16

First steps 20–25
Impressions 20

Destination guide 26–145
San Marco 26
San Polo and Santa Croce 60
Dorsoduro 74
Cannaregio 94
Castello 104
Venice environs 122

Getting away from it all 146–9

Directory 150–89
Shopping 150
Entertainment 156
Children 160
Sport and leisure 162
Food and drink 164
Accommodation 172
Practical guide 178
Language 184

Index 190–91

Maps
Venice 22–3
San Marco 27
Walk: San Marco 37
Walk: Piazzale to Piazza 53
San Polo and Santa Croce 61
Walk: San Polo and Santa Croce 67
Dorsoduro 75
Walk: Dorsoduro 83
Tour: Grand Canal 93
Cannaregio 95
Castello 105
Walk: Castello 111
Walk: Arsenale and Biennale 117
The Venetian lagoon 123
The mainland 137
Venice transport 186

Features
Venice in peril 11
Carnevale 18
Venice and the Orient 30
Of gondolas and gondoliers 40
The doge: last among equals 46
Renaissance art in Venice 78
Life in the lagoon 132
A galaxy of glass 138

Walks and tours
Walk: San Marco 36
Walk: Piazzale to Piazza 52
Walk: San Polo and Santa Croce 66
Walk: Dorsoduro 82
Tour: Grand Canal 90
Walk: Cannaregio 100
Walk: Castello 110
Walk: Arsenale and Biennale 116
Tour: The Circle Line 126

Introduction

For generations, Venice has captured the imagination of writers, poets and painters. Other beautiful cities have been preserved in rhetoric, but Venice is remarkable in that she survives, albeit precariously, just as the great writers have described her.

Most of the prose is predictably ecstatic, but the city's appeal has not been entirely universal. Historian Edward Gibbon complained of the 'old and in general ill-built houses, ruined pictures and stinking ditches'; D H Lawrence called it an 'abhorrent, green slippery city'. Visitors to Venice today, who have seen palaces of apparent perfection on glossy postcards, can be disillusioned by the reality of crumbling façades, moss-ridden watergates, and the sense of nostalgia that seems to permeate the city.

However, for most visitors, the rich visual feast and the wealth of culture more than compensate for the minor blemishes. The lagoon setting, the blend of East and West, the historic role as a great maritime republic, and the density of art and architecture make Venice geographically, culturally and visually unique.

Perhaps more than any other city, Venice appeals to the romantic imagination. It is small and compact, but because of the ceaseless interplay of sunlight and water on the delicate surfaces, the impressions are forever changing. Even those who think they know it well will find it a city that is bewildering, bewitching, elusive and unreal.

As the high waters in winter flood Piazza San Marco, and the problems of pollution, ecology and declining population continue to threaten Venice's unique heritage, millions of euros are being set aside to save the city. Much of this money has been put towards the controversial dams being built to protect Venice from serious flooding, while other funds have been set aside for the constant restoration work that is required. Whatever efforts are made now, the setting of the city will always contribute to its decay as well as its splendour. One can but hope that for as long as Venice survives – as it has for 13 centuries – it will do so as a living city rather than a relic of its glorious past.

Slick motorboats are today emblematic of the waterway-woven city

The city

A city that is, and always has been, wedded to the sea, Venice was created on a cluster of mudflats, laced by waterways and linked by bridges. From the top of St Mark's campanile, the city and surroundings look much as they did in the great days of the Republic. Historically, Venice may be a shadow of its former self – but geographically and aesthetically, it is still unique.

The lagoon

Capital of the province of Venezia and of the region of the Veneto, Venice lies in the centre of a shallow lagoon, sheltered from the open sea by a chain of sandbanks. The lagoon stretches for some 50km (31 miles) from northeast to southwest and varies in width from 8km (5 miles) to 15km (9 miles). The tides from the Adriatic enter and leave the lagoon through three openings in the ring of islets: the Porto di Lido, the Porto di Malamocco and the Porto di Chioggia. Barriers are being erected at these three entrances to stop the high tides entering the lagoon.

The modern province of Venezia covers the islands in the northern and southern lagoon, the perimeters of the lagoon, and the mainland industrial communities of Mestre and Marghera. Venice lost its island status in 1846 when, in a move which angered conservationists, the mainland railway was brought across to the banks of the Grand Canal. The city's link with the mainland was reinforced by the parallel road link built in 1933. Since Venice has no provision for motorised traffic, vehicles cannot go beyond Piazzale Roma, at the western end of the city.

The city

The historic centre of Venice is made up of more than 100 islands, criss-crossed by canals and connected by around 350 bridges. It sounds large, but the whole area, barring the offshore islands of Giudecca and San Giorgio Maggiore, covers only 7sq km (3sq miles). Only a small part of the city stands on solid ground; the rest is built on billions of wooden timbers driven into the floor of the lagoon. The Salute Church alone is said to stand on more than a million piles. All traffic must, of necessity, go by water, but the layout of streets and the abundance of bridges enable pedestrians to cross the entire city on foot.

There are two main waterways, and the most famous is the Canal Grande

(Grand Canal). Snaking its way right through the heart of Venice, this is in effect the city's High Street. A constantly busy waterway, it is used by barges, gondolas, *vaporetti*, water-taxis, mail boats, police boats and all other craft, apart from ocean-going liners and cargo ships. These larger vessels go through the wider Canale della Giudecca (Giudecca Canal), which divides the city from the island of Giudecca.

Economy

The economic life of the historic centre is largely dependent on tourism and

The *campanile* of San Marco provides fine views of the city and its lagoon

traditional crafts. With nearly 14 million visitors descending on Venice each year, it is not surprising that over half the locals are in tourist-related employment.

Mestre and Marghera, incorporated into the city in 1927, are the main industrial centres of Venezia. Marghera was first established as a petrochemical port and factory complex; after World War II, the area became one of the great harbours of Italy. Today, Marghera's importance lies in its shipbuilding yards and its mechanical, chemical, metallurgical and engineering industries.

Population

The population of the city is now down to half of what it was 50 years ago. From 1981 to 1991, the population of the historic centre of Venice fell from 108,000 to 72,000.

By 1995 the population was a mere 70,000 and the average age was 50. Thousands of Venetians, particularly the young, were forced out because of the spiralling property prices, the high rents, the difficulties in finding jobs and the crippling cost of maintaining old buildings. Two-thirds of the population of Greater Venice moved to dryer houses in mainland communities, notably Mestre.

Today, the population of Venice has further dropped to under 60,000 permanent residents. Many shops have closed, and it is mostly the tourist shops and restaurants that remain open.

History

AD **453**   Attila the Hun invades Italy. Mainlanders seek refuge in the Venetian lagoon.

568–572   The Lombard conquest of north Italy causes a further influx of settlers into the lagoon.

697   Paoluccio Anafesto, first *dux* (or doge in Venetian dialect), is appointed by the Byzantium Empire as leader of the lagoon settlement.

800–1000   A period of expansion of Venice's maritime commerce in the eastern Mediterranean and of the granting of important commercial privileges to the city by the Byzantine Empire.

810   Pepin, son of Charlemagne, conquers Venetia but is repelled by Venice.

811   Under Doge Agnello Participazio, the seat of the Venetian government is moved to the islands of the Rialto.

828   Relics of St Mark are stolen from Alexandria and brought to Venice.

1000   Venice completes her conquest of the Dalmatian Coast under Doge Pietro Orseolo II.

1081–5   The Byzantine Empire, under Alexius I, grants Venice further commercial privileges as a reward for her assistance in repelling the Normans from Byzantine territory.

1177   Peace of Venice. Frederick Barbarossa, the Holy Roman Emperor, acknowledges Pope Alexander III as the true pope and their differences are reconciled.

1202–4   Venice provides ships for the Fourth Crusade, led by the blind doge, Enrico Dandalo. The Venetians divert the Crusade to Constantinople, which is taken by the Crusaders along with other strategic points. The Latin Empire in the East is set up and the Byzantine Empire is divided between the conquerors – three-eighths to Venice, which now has a chain of ports from Dalmatia to the Black Sea.

1355 Marin Falier tries to secure absolute power for himself as doge, fails, and is executed.

1380 Venice's victory over the Genoese at Chioggia marks the end of a long maritime struggle for commercial supremacy in the eastern Mediterranean.

1404–5 Venice takes Padua, Verona and Vicenza from Milan. Start of aggressive mainland policy.

1423–54 Under Doge Foscari, Venice becomes a major power on the mainland, annexing land bounded by the Po, the Adda, the Alps and the Isonzo. This is confirmed by the Peace of Lodi between Venice and Milan in 1454.

1453 Ottoman Turks take Constantinople, heralding the start of the Turkish conquest of Venetian possessions in the Eastern Mediterranean.

1498 Vasco da Gama anchors at Calicut, marking the beginning of the Venetian loss of her virtual monopoly of the spice trade.

1508 The Pope, the Holy Roman Emperor, France and Spain combine against Venice in the League of Cambrai, stripping her of many mainland possessions – most of which are recovered on the break-up of the League.

1529 Charles V of Spain now effectively rules all Italy except Venice, which becomes the seat of Italian culture.

1571 Large Christian fleet, including many Venetian galleys, defeats the Turks at the Battle of Lepanto, checking Turkish expansion into the Western Mediterranean.

1606–7 Led by Paolo Sarpi, Venice defies Pope Paul V's demand to exercise judicial authority in Venice.

1630 Bubonic plague reduces the population by nearly 50,000.

1669	Turks take Crete from Venice.
1684–99	War of the Holy League ends in Christian gains and the recovery of the Peloponnese from Turkey.
1715	Turks reconquer the Peloponnese, later confirmed by the Treaty of Passarowitz (1718).
1779	Enfeebled by her loss of empire and stripped of political and commercial influence, Venice 'seems to have become a marionette theatre' (Gradenigo).
1797	Venice surrenders to Napoleon, ending the 1,000-year-old Venetian Republic.
1815	Treaty of Vienna places the Veneto under Austrian control.
1848–9	Under Daniele Manin, Venice revolts against Austrian rule, but is forced to yield after a sustained siege.
1866	Veneto is unified with Italy after an Italo-Prussian army defeats the Austrians at Sadowa.
1920s & 1930s	Industrial zone at Marghera constructed.
1966	Catastrophic floods lead to the launch of international funds to restore the city.
1988	First stage of the lagoon flood barrier prototype (MOSE) completed.
1996	La Fenice opera house devastated by fire.
2004	La Fenice reopened. Work started on MOSE.
2006	Palazzo Grassi reopens.
2008	Ponte della Costituzione, designed by Spanish architect Santiago Calatrava, officially opens. It is the fourth bridge to span the Grand Canal, connecting the rail and road termini. In December, Venice suffers its worst flooding in 22 years, with waters rising 1.56m (5ft).
2009	The Punta della Dogana contemporary arts centre opens in June.
2010	In March, Venice votes for a new left-wing mayor, Giorgio Orsoni.

Venice in peril

On 4 and 5 November 1966, high tides swept into the lagoon, flooding the city's squares and alleys. Oil spilled out from broken storage tanks, black waters gushed into ground floors and the Piazzetta was under 1.2m (4ft) of water for several hours. The problem of *acqua alta* (high water) is as old as the city, but its increased frequency led to an international appeal. Under UNESCO, some 30 organisations were set up to save the city.

The Consorzio Venezia Nuova, a group of engineering companies licensed to carry out the programme of sea and flood defence, is convinced that the only solution is a mobile barrier system that would separate the sea from the lagoon. The prototype, MOSE (Modulo Sperimentale Elettromeccanico), has been approved, but this multi-million euro project has met strong opposition from Italia Nostra and the Greens. Work has started, with a deadline penned in for 2014, though it is unlikely to be completed until well into this century. Meanwhile, defences have been set up to lessen the force of the tides, and a major programme for dredging the canals and maintaining the eroding foundations has been initiated. These measures did not, however, save the city from its worst flooding in over 20 years, when in December 2009 water levels rose to 1.56m (5ft) higher than the norm, causing millions of euros of damage.

Floods are not the only threat to the city's unique heritage. Pollution from chemical plants at Marghera and industrial waste from the Adriatic have also had ruinous effects.

According to official surveys, the waters are a lot cleaner than they were ten years ago. As for the centuries-old problem of Venice sinking, this was alleviated by measures taken in the 1970s against industrial communities disturbing the balance of the lagoon.

Flooding of the Grand Canal, pollution and rising damp have caused incalculable damage

Politics

The decaying city is dogged by the centralised political structure, and it has slowly seen a decline in its living community. The administration faces a huge backlog of crises which it has been struggling to overcome. Among these are the exodus of Venetians to the mainland, the dearth of decent housing, the dredging of canals, the reconstruction of foundations and the inactivity of the industrial zone of Marghera.

Italian political system

Italy is a parliamentary democracy with a republican constitution. The head of state is the president of the Republic, who nominates a prime minister. Since World War II, the country has largely been ruled by a series of short-lived coalition governments.

The town hall – at the heart of Venetian politics

The Christian Democrats have been dominant, but the avalanche of corruption scandals in 1993 led to their downfall. The first centre-left coalition since World War II, the 'Olive Tree', dominated by the Democratic Left Party (PDS), led the country into the European Union. Italian politics subsequently underwent an abrupt about-face in 2001, and a three-party right-wing grouping, headed by media magnate Silvio Berlusconi, was returned. He was replaced by centre-left former prime minister Romano Prodi in 2006, only to return to power when Prodi's government collapsed in April 2008.

The political scene in Venice

In Venice, after two successful terms in office, widely admired mayor-cum-philosopher Massimo Cacciari from the centre-left resigned and handed over the reins to his successor Paolo Costa in 2001. Cacciari had initiated major efforts towards converting Venice from being the most archaic city in Europe to the 'first Post-Modern community'.

A university professor in economics, Costa encouraged investment and research bodies in Venice to continue the reverse exodus of people and businesses. New residences were developed in the historic city centre and on the island of Giudecca.

Massimo Cacciari returned as mayor in 2005 but stood down before the administrative elections in 2010, when fellow left-winger and erstwhile lawyer Giorgio Orsoni became mayor of the lagoon city.

Tourist culture versus city life

While the economy of Venice depends on the tourist industry, the city has neither the space nor the facilities to cope with the deluge of visitors in high season. Because of this, EXPO 2000 was not held in the Veneto, though some believed that it would have boosted the economy and encouraged necessary services to the city.

To improve transport, a light railway system has been proposed to link Padua, Mestre/Venice and Treviso – and the old idea of a sub-lagoon metro is often aired.

Politics

The Lion of San Marco, symbol of Venice, became famous throughout the world

Culture

Once a great maritime republic, brokering the commodities of the West for the luxuries of the East, Venice's rich cultural heritage reflects a remarkable diversity of influences. When the Republic fell in 1797, however, the city became something of a living museum. In recent years it is thanks to a Frenchman, Francois Pinault, that Venice has enjoyed a cultural boost, with the reopening of Palazzo Grassi and the opening of Punta della Dogana, both containing prestigious works from his vast private collection.

The fabric of the city

The city's trading links with the East had a marked impact on early buildings such as the Cathedral of Torcello and the Basilica of San Marco, but the essence of Venice resides most eloquently in the canal façades of the palaces built in the unique Venetian Gothic style. The two great architectural geniuses of the Venetian Renaissance, Coducci and Sansovino, used Renaissance forms but subtly adapted them to the spirit of the city so that light, airiness and intricate texture prevailed. Pietro Lombardo and his sons sculpted marble façades and statues, and added characteristic richness to the buildings.

In the 16th century, Palladio made his essential classical contribution with two great churches on the islands of southern Venice.

Longhena brought pomp and gravitas with his monumental Baroque structures of the 17th century. It was in this epoch that the city effectively became the complex and sophisticated place we see today.

A city of art and music

Venetian painting flourished potently from the 1450s to the end of the 16th century. The Renaissance, which was already well established in Florence, was given new impetus by five great resident Venetian painters: Giovanni Bellini, Giorgione, Titian, Tintoretto and Veronese. In the 18th century, while the rest of Italy stagnated, Venetian decorative art flourished, and Venetian-born Tiepolo led the field in Europe.

As commerce declined in Venice, music became part of her lifeblood. Claudio Monteverdi made the city the home of opera, a tradition which continued right through to the 19th century when the beautiful Fenice theatre saw premieres of some of Rossini's and Verdi's great operas. The Fenice burnt down in 1996 but was rebuilt (and reopened in 2004), as it was after fires in 1792 and 1836. Luigi Nono, the renowned composer of atonal music, was born here, and a music foundation in his name can be found on the island of Giudecca. Meanwhile, the Biennale organises an international music festival every autumn.

The Venice of today

Lack of space, combined with the conservative Venetian character, largely precluded the intrusion of modern buildings into the city. The stark 1960s' buildings of the Hotel Bauer Grünwald

A gondolier takes a break between customers

and the Cassa di Risparmio in Campo Manin were seen as scandals and, consequently, the emphasis since then has largely been on the preservation or renovation of the old rather than the construction of the new.

Venice itself is not renowned for its modern artists, but every other year contemporary culture hits the city in the form of the Biennale. The event now embraces architecture, theatre, music, dance and cinema, as well as painting, sculpture and video forms. The main venue is the Giardini Pubblici, where more than 50 countries have pavilions. Further exhibitions are housed in the Arsenale Corderie and venues all over town. Occasionally, some huge, eye-catching exhibit is set conspicuously along the Grand Canal or in the lagoon to remind the tourists that there is more to Venice than ancient palaces.

The Biennale organises the Venice Film Festival, which was established in 1932. Showing a great range of films from all around the world, the event brings stars and *paparazzi* to the Lido. Though not quite the glamorous event it was in the post-war years, the festival seems to be making a comeback.

Modern culture apart, Venice offers a wide choice of art exhibitions in palaces and galleries, a range of concerts and opera (held in the magnificent Malibran theatre as well as La Fenice), and a staggering wealth of permanent art in its museums, churches and palaces.

Festivals

The Venetians still have a genuine love of pageantry. Most of the fiestas are long-established events, with their roots deep in Venetian history. The most spectacular among them are the Carnevale, the Festa del Redentore, the Regata Storica and the Vogalonga.

February/March

Celebrations in costumes and masks at the **Venice Carnevale**. Exact dates for the Carnevale (*see pp18–19*) are available from Italian State Tourist offices.

May

The **Vogalonga**, held on a Sunday in May (the date changes from year to year), is a marathon regatta open to anyone with a rowing boat. The course is 32km (20 miles) long, running from Sant'Elena at the eastern end of the city across the lagoon to Burano, and then back to Venice along the Canale di Cannaregio, then the Grand Canal.

The **Festa della Sensa** on Ascension Day celebrates the annual occasion on which the doge would be rowed to the Lido in his ceremonial barge, the Bucintoro, to cast a ring into the sea. This event symbolised the marriage of the city to the sea. Today it is re-enacted (albeit on a less spectacular scale) with the mayor acting as the doge.

June

The **Biennale**, which is one of the largest international exhibitions of contemporary art in the world, takes place from June until October in odd-numbered years. Exhibitions are held in the national pavilions of the Giardini Pubblici (Public Gardens) and also in the Arsenale and other venues throughout the city. The Biennale also organises the **International Film Festival** (*see opposite*) and a host of other events, including dance, music and drama, in addition to the art exhibitions. The centenary of the Biennale was celebrated in 1995.

July

One of the most colourful occasions of the year is the **Festa del Redentore**, held on the third Sunday of July in thanksgiving for the ending of the plague in 1576 (*see p123*). A pontoon of boats is built across the Giudecca Canal, linking up the Zattere to the Redentore Church on the island of Giudecca.

On the Saturday night, hundreds of Venetians take to the water in their garlanded boats, while others wine, dine and make merry on rafts and ferries put out for the *festa*. The climax is a fantastic firework display which bursts over the lagoon.

August/September

The **International Film Festival**, organised by the Biennale, takes place at Palazzo del Cinema and other venues on the Lido at the end of August/ beginning of September.

An exotic Carnevale disguise

The oldest and one of the most important film festivals in Europe, it lasts for two weeks and films are shown day and night. For information, contact Venice Biennale (*tel: 041 521 8711. www.labiennale.org*).

The first Sunday in September sees the spectacular **Regata Storica**. Festivities consist of a splendid Grand Canal procession of traditional vessels and a series of boat races along the course of the canal. The most popular and competitive of these are the gondolier races, each boat or team representing its island or district.

October/November

The **Venice Marathon** is held in late October starting at Stra on the Brenta canal to conclude 42km (26 miles) later near San Marco.

The main event of the season is the **Festa della Salute**, which, like the Festa del Redentore, has its roots in an outbreak of the plague. On 21 November, a pontoon bridge is built across the Grand Canal to the Salute and it is the one time in the year when you can enter the church by the main doors.

The Azienda di Promozione Turistica di Venezia (*Castello 4421. Tel: 041 529 8711. www.turismovenezia.it*) publishes a bimonthly magazine *Leo Bussola*, giving the dates of all festivals and events. Information is also available from the tourist offices at Piazza San Marco and the railway station.

Carnevale

The 18th century was the great age of the Venetian Carnival. Celebrations started on 26 December and carried on until Shrove Tuesday. It was a riotous affair, the anonymity of the mask giving free rein to fantasies, passions, debauchery and roguery. Wild and exotic animals from far-flung countries were brought to Piazza San Marco, theatres became gambling houses, men dressed up as women and their wives mingled with harlots. Social distinctions were thrown to the wind and characters were well and truly incognito, from the doge down to the beggars.

The revelries came to an abrupt halt under Napoleon. Half-hearted

Carnival mask

carnivals occasionally took place in the 19th century, but it was not until the 1970s that the event was officially reinstated – this time primarily as a tourist attraction.

Though tame when compared with its 18th-century counterpart, and lasting a mere ten days, it is one of the most exotic and colourful events in Europe. Foreigners flock to the city to partake in the party. Dazzling amounts of money are spent on costumes and masks, and preparations start months before the event. One participant may have as many as three costumes, while others may come in pairs or groups, with matching costumes.

In 2010, Venice Carnival was officially cited as the most popular live/televised event in Italy. Confirming its worldwide popularity, the carnival was used to promote Italy at the 2010 Shanghai Expo, with performers parading through the streets, dressed in Renaissance garb and brandishing Venetian Serenissima flags.

The merriment goes on day and night, the city becoming a stage set for pageants, parades, plays and private parties in *palazzi* (palaces). Revellers fill the squares and take to the waterways, gliding in gondolas and creating a riot of colour along the dark canals. The festivities culminate on Shrove Tuesday with a masked ball, and often a procession of boats gliding down the candlelit Grand Canal.

To reap the benefits of the hordes that descend on the city, most of the hotels in Venice now stay open for the winter and put up their prices for Carnival. If you are planning on going, book well in advance. (*For ideas on disguises, see pp154–5.*)

Carnival figures re-create the medieval age; months of work go into the creation of exotic costumes

Impressions

Once did She hold the gorgeous east in fee;
And was the safeguard of the west: the worth
Of Venice did not fall below her birth,
Venice, the eldest Child of Liberty.

William Wordsworth, *On the Extinction of*
the Venetian Republic, 1802

When to go

Venice has become an all-year-round tourist destination, the only really quiet times being November, early December and January. The peak season runs from June to the end of September, with July and August being the worst months, with heat, mosquitoes, crowds and canal odours. Weatherwise, the ideal months are May, September and October, during which time it is usually warm and sunny. From late autumn, there is always the risk of *acqua alta*, the high tides that submerge the Piazza and other parts of the city. Winters can be cold and foggy – or romantically misty, depending on your mood.

Off-season advantages are the absence of crowds and the substantial discounts offered by hotels, particularly upmarket ones. However, this does not apply to the festive days of the Carnevale (lasting ten days up to Shrove Tuesday), when the city is thronged by masked revellers – and the prices match those during the peak season.

Arrival and bearings

The most spectacular and appropriate way to arrive in Venice is via the lagoon. This you can do if you arrive by air and take the bâteau-mouche-like launch from Marco Polo airport across the lagoon to a handful of destinations around the city (*see www.alilaguna.it for details*). From here you are either at the mercy of money-grabbing porters or water-taxis, or you trust your judgement and your map of Venice, board a *vaporetto* or weave your way through the maze of alleys to find your hotel. The much cheaper alternative from the airport is a land bus to Piazzale Roma, from where there is a good waterbus service to most parts of the city and porters if you want them.

For first-time visitors, it may take a while to adjust to the traffic-free streets. It is one of the great joys of Venice that you can stroll anywhere in the city and forget the noise of cars and the inconvenience of crossing streets.

Sightseeing

It is not only the treasures of the museums and galleries which make up the artistic heritage of the city. Churches all over Venice are rich repositories of art, though not conspicuously so. It is not unusual to find a dusty Titian or Tintoretto tucked away in a dark corner or sacristy of a church. Many of these paintings are impossible to see without using the mechanical lighting systems. Sightseers should therefore go equipped with a pocketful of coins, which are also useful for the translated commentaries in the bigger churches.

Venetians respect their heritage, and most of their churches have notices requesting visitors to dress suitably, maintain silence and behave in a respectful manner. Sightseeing during services is discouraged. Most churches now either charge an entrance fee (the Basilica itself is free, though the Pala d'Oro, Treasury and Museum charge admission fees), or encourage you to leave a donation.

A convenient aid to visiting Venice is the Venice Card, available for one, three or seven days. It covers transport and sightseeing and can be pre-booked. Visit *www.venicecard.com*

Particular to Venice are the *scuole*, or confraternities, which were founded here during the Middle Ages. These institutions were set up under the auspices of a saint for religious or charitable purposes, or for the protection of common interests. Thanks to generous donations, the *scuole* amassed sufficient funds to commission leading artists to decorate their headquarters. Many of these works of art can still be seen today.

Gondolas, symbols of Venice

Venice town plan (*for Tour route see pp126–7*)

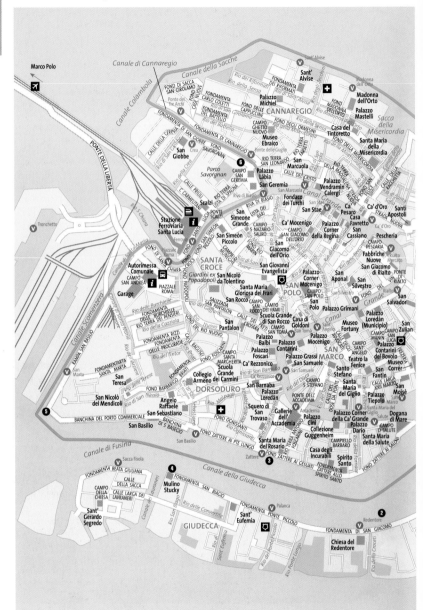

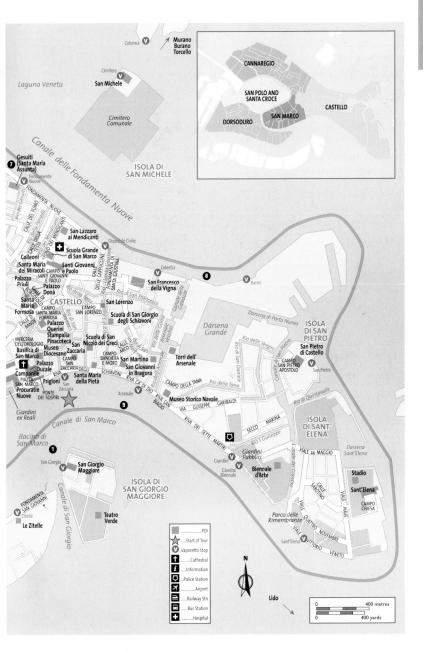

Colonna

Murano
Burano
Torcello

Cimitero

San Michele

Laguna Veneta

Cimitero
Comunale

ISOLA DI
SAN MICHELE

CANNAREGIO

SAN POLO AND
SANTA CROCE

CASTELLO

SAN MARCO

DORSODURO

Canale delle Fondamenta Nuove

Gesuiti
(Santa Maria
Assunta)
Fondamente
Nuove

FONDAMENTA NUOVE

San Lazzaro
ai Mendicanti

Scuola Grande
di San Marco

Colleoni

Ospedale Civile

Santa Maria
dei Miracoli

Santi Giovanni
e Paolo

Celestia

Bacini

Palazzo
Priuli

SANTI GIOVANNI
E PAOLO

Palazzo
Donà

San Francesco
della Vigna

Santa
Maria
Formosa

CASTELLO

San Lorenzo

Rio di San Francesco

CAMPO
SANTA MARIA
FORMOSA

CAMPO
SAN LORENZO

Palazzo
Querini
Stampalia
Pinacoteca

Scuola di San Giorgio
degli Schiavoni

Dàrsena
Grande

Darsena di Porta Nuovo

ISOLA
DI SAN
PIETRO

MERCERIA
DELL'OROLOGIO

Museo
Diocesano

Scuola di San
Nicolò dei Greci

San Pietro
di Castello

Basilica di
San Marco

Palazzo
Ducale

CAMPO
SAN
ZACCARIA

San Martino

San Giovanni
in Bragora

Torri dell'
Arsenale

Rio delle Vergini

Rio di San Pietro

CAMPO
SAN PIETRO
APOSTOLO

San Pietro

Campanile

Prigioni

PIAZZA
SAN MARCO

Procuratie
Nuove

RIVA
DEGLI
SCHIAVONI

Santa Maria
della Pietà

San
Zaccaria

PONTE
DEI SOSPIRI

Arsenale

RIVA CA' DI DIO

Rio della Tana

CAMPO DELLA TANA

Rio di Quintavalle

Giardini
ex Reali

Canale di San Marco

Museo Storico Navale

VIA GIUSEPPE GARIBALDI

ISOLA
DI SANT'
ELENA

Bacino di
San Marco

RIVA DEI SETTE MARTIRI

MARINA

Rio s' Giuseppe

SECCO

Darsena
Sant'Elena

San Giorgio

San Giorgio
Maggiore

Giardini

Giardini
Biennale

Giardini
Pubblici

Biennale
d'Arte

VIALE 24 MAGGIO

Stadio

Sant'Elena

FONDAMENTA
SAN GIOVANNI

Zitelle

ISOLA DI
SAN GIORGIO
MAGGIORE

Teatro
Verde

Parco delle
Rimembranze

CAMPO
CHIESA

CALLE SABOTINO

VIALE QUATTRO NOVEMBRE

VIALE PIAVE

Le Zitelle

Sant'Elena

VITTORIO

VENETO

	POI
☆	Start of Tour
Ⓥ	Vaporetto Stop
✝	Cathedral
i	Information
	Police Station
✈	Airport
	Railway Stn
	Bus Station
✚	Hospital

N

0   400 metres

0   400 yards

Lido

The layout of Venice

First-time visitors invariably lose their way in the maze of little alleys. However, the city is surprisingly small (crossing it from north to south takes no more than 40 minutes) and you are rarely far from the yellow signs indicating the main landmarks of Piazza San Marco, the railway station and the Rialto. The Canal Grande (Grand Canal), which cuts through the city in an inverted S shape, provides another invaluable landmark. The canal is spanned by four bridges: the Scalzi, near the station, the Rialto, roughly halfway along, the Accademia, between the Rialto and San Marco, and the Costituzione, between the railway station and the bus terminus. The last – designed by leading Spanish architect Santiago Calatrava – finally opened in 2008 after being dogged by delays for years. At other points you can cross by *traghetto* (*see below*).

The city is divided into six administrative districts, called *sestieri*: San Marco, San Polo, Santa Croce, Dorsoduro, Cannaregio and Castello.

Beyond the city are the islands of the northern and southern lagoon. Murano, Burano and Torcello are reached by public waterbus, and the Lido, Venice's beach resort, is linked to the city by regular boat services.

Getting around

By gondola

These days this quintessential Venetian craft exists solely for the pleasure of tourists. There is nothing more memorable (apart from the charges of the gondolier) than to glide along the city's winding canals.

To avoid paying more than the already exorbitant charges, start by establishing the official charges (*see pp183–6*) – and be prepared to bargain.

By *traghetto*

Crossing the Grand Canal at six different points, the *traghetti* provide the cheapest gondola rides in the city. The points of the crossings are indicated on most good maps of Venice. The boat is manned by two gondoliers, one at either end of the boat, and the passengers normally stand for the journey. Services run from early morning to early afternoon or all day, depending on the point of crossing.

By waterbus

The waterbuses, or *vaporetti*, provide a scenic and entertaining way of getting around Venice and out to the islands. Originally steam-powered (*vaporetto* means 'little steamer'), today they are diesel-run, flat-keeled motorboats. Strictly speaking, the word *vaporetto* refers only to the wider of the boats, such as the No 1 that takes the slow route down the Grand Canal. The thinner, faster boats are the *motoscafi*, which go at a licking pace.

Tickets are sold at most landing stages, some bars, tobacconists and other outlets displaying the ACTV sign. Rover tickets, available for periods from 12 hours to seven days, are good value for money.

By water-taxi

These sleek, varnished motorboats are strictly the domain of the rich. The booklet *Un Ospite di Venezia* (*www. unospitedivenezia.it*) lists the taxi ranks and the official prices for journeys within the city and to the islands.

Culture and customs

In a city so accustomed to visitors, tourism is very much a way of life. In high season, there are more tourists than local residents, so as a foreigner you are unlikely to feel ill-at-ease. It is worth remembering, however, that Italians are strict on the dress code in churches. In order not to give offence, avoid bare shoulders and scanty shorts.

Smoking is now forbidden in all public places, including on the *vaporetti* and at *vaporetto* stops. But you can smoke at outdoor tables in bars and restaurants.

To Venetians, as to most Italians, appearances are all-important and you will rarely see a badly dressed or scruffy local. Shop windows have exquisite displays and any item purchased is likely to be beautifully wrapped.

You pay for it all, of course, and the high prices in Venice – higher than in any other city in Italy – are a cause of perpetual complaint from visitors and locals alike. This is nothing new, however. The merchants of Venice were fleecing foreigners from the earliest days of her great mercantile empire.

Impressions

The bustling streets and waterways of Venice

San Marco

The first and foremost of the city's six sestieri – *not only because of the wealth of architectural and artistic treasures it contains, but also because it was the seat of power both in Venice and throughout the vast Serenissima empire. From this district, wars were waged, crusades coordinated and political pacts forged. Nowadays, this district is bursting with centuries-old loot, and is the place to go for all the big names in Italian fashion.*

Basilica di San Marco (St Mark's Basilica)

Dominating the Piazza, the Basilica di San Marco is a symbol of Venetian glory. Embellished and enriched over the centuries with loot from the East, it is a huge, complex and mysterious edifice – as much a museum as a church. It has provoked more comment than any other building in Venice, occasionally been dismissed as barbaric, but more often praised to the skies.

Legend has it that in 828, two Venetian merchants forced their way into a church in Alexandria in Egypt, stole the corpse of St Mark and brought it back to Venice. By 832, a church had been built to enshrine the relic. In 976, during a riot against the tyranny of Doge Pietro Candiano IV, a fire broke out in the Ducal Palace and destroyed the church, along with the saint's relics.

Within two years, another church had been built in its place. By the 11th century, when Venice had truly come of age, this was pulled down and replaced by a third, larger, more lavish edifice. This is the church you see today, albeit with many later additions and alterations.

The Basilica cannot be covered comfortably in one visit. Ideally, you should make several short visits, perhaps at different times of day: in the early morning, during Mass or when the church is illuminated. In the summer months you will almost inevitably share the church with hordes of tour groups following their guides. The best times to avoid the day-trippers are as soon as the doors open at 9.30am, and in the early evening when the crowds have departed.

Façade

Once faced in plain brick, the exterior was later encrusted with mosaics, marbles and carvings. Despite the obviously Gothic carvings, the Basilica still has the appearance of a Byzantine church. Five cupolas were added in the 13th century, and there are five portals,

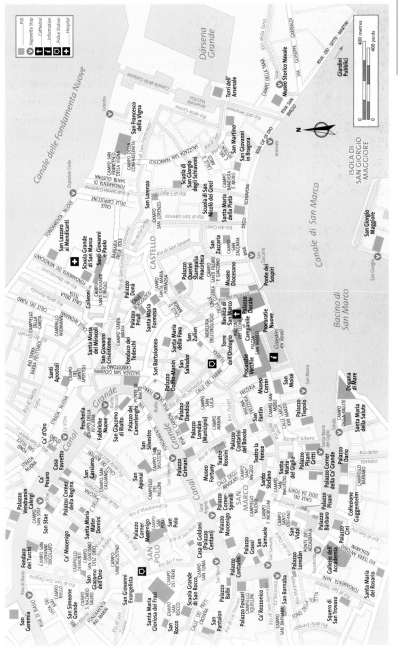

San Marco

the arches of which are decorated with glistening mosaics.

The only original mosaic on the exterior is the one above the Porta di San Alipio, on the far left. This portrays *The Translation of the Body of the Saint to the Church of San Marco* (1260–70), and you can see how the Basilica looked in the 13th century.

The lunettes over the next portal and the two beyond the central doorway depict further scenes from the legend of

St Mark. These are 17th- and 18th-century reworkings of 13th-century mosaics and bear no comparison to the Porta di San Alipio mosaic.

The mosaic in the central arch dates from the 19th century and shows *Christ in Glory* and *The Last Judgement*. On the upper level, seen from the left, the 17th-century mosaics depict *The Deposition*, *The Descent from the Cross*, *The Resurrection* and *The Ascension*.

The four horses above the main portal are copies of the originals which are now housed in the Marciano Museum (*see p32*). The portal, flanked by marble columns, is decorated with finely carved 13th- and 14th-century bas-reliefs showing both Eastern and Western influences. Look carefully to see animals fighting and scenes of daily life (inner arch), the months, the signs of the zodiac, the Virtues and the Beatitudes (middle arch), Venetian trades, and Christ and the Prophets (outer arch).

At the corner by the Doge's Palace, the mysterious and charming figures of 'The Tetrarchs', more familiarly known as 'The Moors', are thought to have come from Syria in the 4th century.

In front of the Baptistery door, the finely carved 'Pillars of Acre' were believed, until recently, to have been taken from Acre in Palestine when it fell to the Crusaders in 1258. Research now confirms that these came from a church in Constantinople and were taken, along with all the other loot, in 1204.

Details on the façade of the Basilica di San Marco

Atrium

Scantily dressed visitors do not get beyond the custodian who stands in the atrium, turning away bare midriffs, mini skirts and short shorts.

The atrium mosaics, depicting scenes from the Old Testament, are some of the finest and oldest in the Basilica. Follow them from right to left, starting with *The Genesis Cupola*, depicting in concentric circles 24 episodes of the *Creation of the World*. This is followed in the first arch by stories of Noah and the Flood.

In the second arch, the Noah theme continues: scenes of Noah quaffing wine in the vineyard, his son Ham showing his nakedness to his brothers, and Noah being buried. The figures of the *Virgin with Apostles and Saints*, either side of the central doorway, are the oldest in the Basilica, dating from the 11th century.

Interior

At first glance, the interior appears huge, cavernous and daunting, but when your eyes grow accustomed to the dim light, the Basilica becomes exotic, even intimate. The overall effect of the marble and mosaics, the columns and the cupolas is unmistakably Byzantine, and it is easy to see why it is called the Basilica d'Oro (Basilica of Gold). Unless the church is illuminated, the only light comes from the flickering lamps and the rays of sunlight from the cupola windows which gleam on patches of mosaic on the *pavimento* and walls.

The mysterious light enhances the religious message of San Marco's interior

There are over 4,000sq m (43,056sq ft) of mosaics, covering vaults, arches and domes. In the early days, mosaicists were lured from the East to decorate the church, but the Venetians soon learnt the craft and continued to embellish the Basilica, introducing Western influences. The earliest mosaics are 12th and 13th century, though most of these were restored in the 17th and 18th centuries.

Splendid examples of some of the oldest mosaics are the *Pentecost Dome*, first cupola along the nave, and the *Ascension of Christ* in the central dome. Other early mosaics are the four saints in the dome over the right transept, the magnificent figures of the *Virgin and Prophets* in the right aisle, and, on the wall above, the scenes of the *Agony in the Garden*.

(*Cont. on p32*)

Venice and the Orient

During the earliest days of her history, Venice was no more than the rump of the Byzantine Empire in Italy. Until 828, when the relics of St Mark were smuggled into the city, her patron saint was a Greek, St Theodore, whose statue stands on top of one of the lofty columns of the Piazzetta.

It was when St Mark became her patron saint that Venice began to assert her independence. By 1081 her navy was so powerful that Emperor Alexius Comnenus appealed to her to eject the Normans from Byzantine lands. In doing so, Venice exacted a high price. The city was granted unparalleled trading privileges and was exempt from all taxes throughout the eastern empire.

In 1204, Venice diverted the Fourth Crusade to Constantinople and helped to set up the Latin Empire in the East. In doing so, she not only carried off a vast loot but also annexed 'a quarter and half a quarter' of Byzantine lands. In 1380 she rounded off her equity in the East with a resounding victory over her great naval rival, Genoa. Venice now had the monopoly on spices, which she sold to Northern and Western Europe at extortionate prices. The Venetian warehouses, some of which still exist, were packed with exotic spices, silks, precious stones and perfumes.

The flavour of the East also manifested itself in the buildings of Venice. The design, dome and mosaics of the Basilica San Marco are all expressions of the spirit of Byzantium – indeed, much of San Marco is made up of Eastern plunder. Many of the elegant palaces along the Grand Canal, built by the great merchant and patrician dynasties, are distinctly oriental, while the so-called 'Venetian Gothic' structures, such as the famous Ca' d'Oro, are subtle and brilliant derivations of the styles that Venetian architects had inherited from Byzantium. These buildings are the very essence of Venice and give the city its unmistakable oriental flavour.

The flavour of Byzantium in the domes of the Basilica San Marco

Gothic pinnacles vie with the oriental cupola of the Madonna dell'Orto

Marciano Museum

Steep steps from the atrium lead up to a museum containing works of art, fragments of mosaic, tapestries, lace and other items linked to the history of the Basilica.

The prize exhibits are the four horses in gilded bronze, which were part of the booty taken during the Fourth Crusade. This spirited team of four has travelled a great deal since their creation: from Rome to Constantinople to Venice, to Paris (pinched by Napoleon), back to Venice, to Rome again and, finally (one assumes), to Venice. The horses which once adorned the façade were brought inside because of the steady erosion outside from pollution and pigeon droppings. Goethe, who of course saw the horses *in situ*, commented,

'What seemed strange to me was, that closely viewed they appear heavy, while from the Piazza below they look light as deer.'

The gallery in the museum is the best place to view the whole Basilica. From here, you can see the Greek-cross plan of the church, the marble pillars, the mosaics and the *matronei*, or women's galleries, where females would attend services separated from men, in accordance with Greek Orthodox custom.

The external balcony, or Loggia dei Cavalli, provided a grandstand view of the Piazza activities for the doge, his senators and visiting dignitaries. To the left there are bird's-eye views of the Piazzetta with its soaring granite columns.

The Basilica San Marco: a private 'chapel' to the doges for almost a thousand years

Pala d'Oro/Chancel/Iconostasis

A focal point of the Basilica, though only conspicuous because of the long queues to view it, is the precious Pala d'Oro behind the altar. This jewel-studded altarpiece was commissioned in Constantinople in 976, and remodelled over the centuries.

Although Napoleon took his pick of the jewels, there are still around 2,000 left, including pearls, sapphires, emeralds, garnets, amethysts and enamels. (For a ticket, follow the flow through St Clement Chapel, on the right of the rood screen.)

Also in the chancel, above the altar, is a *baldacchino* (altar canopy), supported by alabaster columns carved with scenes from the New Testament. The bronze figures of *The Evangelists* on the balustrade are by Sansovino, as are the bronze reliefs of the *Scenes from the Life of St Mark* on the walls either side of the altar.

Separating the chancel from the nave is the Byzantine iconostasis, or roodscreen, surmounted by Gothic marble statues of the Apostles and the Madonna. These were the work of the Masegne brothers, who were the leading sculptors of the early 15th century.

Pavimento (floor)

Like a huge, gently undulating oriental carpet, the mosaic floor is decorated with complex geometric designs and allegorical representations of animals and birds. Fragments of the original floor still exist, such as scenes of a lion biting a wolf, an eagle attacking a wild animal, and a swan with a serpent in its beak.

Left transept

The east chapel in the left transept contains the much-venerated *Madonna of Nicopeia*. Yet another trophy from the Fourth Crusade, this was a precious icon which was carried at the head of the Eastern emperor's army.

At the end of the left transept, the Chapel of St Isidore contains the saint's relics. The 14th-century mosaics on the walls depict episodes from his life, including the stealing of his body from Chios and its transferral to Venice. To the left of Isidore's Chapel is the Chapel of the Mascoli (Men), so called because of the confraternity of males who used to worship here.

Treasury

Entered from the right transept, the treasury is devoted to booty plundered from Byzantium: sacred Byzantine icons, goblets studded with gems, and precious vessels displayed in glass cases. Worth singling out is the 11th-century embossed silver-gilt Pyx – a container in the shape of a five-domed oriental basilica – used to preserve Communion bread.

Baptistery

The Baptistery was closed for a number of years for restoration work. The splendid ceiling mosaics show scenes from the *Life of Christ* and the *Life of John the Baptist*. Many doges have tombs here, including Andrea Dandolo (d.1354), the commissioner of the mosaics and the last doge to be buried in the Basilica: future doges were buried in the Church of Santi Giovanni e Paolo (*see pp113–14*). Jacopo Sansovino, sculptor and state architect of Venice, designed the font (1545) and is buried in front of the altar.

Zen Chapel

Next to the Baptistery, and also fully restored, the Zen Chapel once formed part of the atrium. It was built in the early 16th century by Cardinal Giambattista Zen, who bequeathed his estate to Venice with the proviso that he would be buried in San Marco. Hence his mighty monument, decorated with

putti (cherubs) and six figures representing the virtues. The tomb and altar were the combined work of Alessandro Leopardi, Antonio Lombardo and Paolo Savin.

For the Campanile of San Marco and the Torre dell'Orologio (Clock Tower), see pp50–51 & p56 respectively.

The Basilica is in Piazza San Marco. Tel: 041 270 8311. www.basilicasanmarco.it. Basilica open: Mon–Sat 9.45am–5.30pm, Sun & public holidays 2–5pm. Free admission. Museum open: daily 9.45am–4.45pm. Treasury & Pala d'Oro open: same as Basilica. Admission charge. Mass: Mon–Sat hourly 7am–noon & 6.45pm, Sun hourly 7–9am, 10.30am & noon. The church is illuminated daily 11.30am–12.30pm, Sat afternoons & Sun & feast days.

Inspiring frescoes adorn the Basilica's façade

Accademia Bridge on the Grand Canal frames the distant Salute

Canal Grande (Grand Canal)

Described as 'the finest street in the world', the Grand Canal sweeps majestically through the heart of the city, providing a dazzling array of more than 100 palace façades. Known to the locals as the Canalazzo, it is nearly 4km (2½ miles) long, stretching in an inverted S shape from Piazzale Roma to San Marco. The waterway teems with traffic, from skiffs and gondolas to waterbuses and launches. For those accustomed to terra firma, it is a novelty to see the post carried on a red motorboat, crates of radicchio arriving by boat at the Rialto, and bundles of hotel sheets on the laundry barge.

The palaces and houses flanking the canal range from the finely restored to the sadly dilapidated. First-time visitors who have only seen Venice through postcards and photographs may well be taken aback by the peeling façades; but while such sites may offend elsewhere, the decay in Venice seems to go hand in hand with its beauty. No one can deny that a journey down this waterway is one of the world's most delightful experiences.

Every palace on the Grand Canal tells a story: home to a doge, birthplace of a composer, residence of an artist or rendezvous of the literati. Royalty have stayed here, doges have died here. During the days of the Republic, all the mansions were private residences and all were called ca', short for casa,

(*Cont. on p38*)

Walk: San Marco

This walk will familiarise first-time visitors to Venice with the most famous sestiere *of this city, which, one might say, is designed for walkers. Piazza San Marco (see pp49–56) and the Basilica (see pp26–34) are described in detail elsewhere.*

Allow 1½ to 2 hours.

Start at the Merceria dell'Orologio by the Clock Tower in Piazza San Marco.

1 Merceria

The English diarist, John Evelyn, described the Merceria in 1645 as 'The most delicious streete in the World'. He wrote of the sumptuous damasks and silks, the apothecary shops, perfumers and countless cages of nightingales. The Merceria is still the main shopping thoroughfare of the city.
Follow the Merceria towards the Rialto. At the Church of San Salvatore, turn right and stop at the next square.

2 Campo San Bartolomeo

Goldoni's smiling statue lends a cheerful air to an otherwise ordinary square. The statue has always been a favourite rendezvous, particularly for young Venetians.

3 Rialto

Stalls selling silk, glass and trinkets start at the foot of the bridge. Walk up for a bird's-eye view of the Grand Canal, seen from balustrades on either side. On the far side of the Rialto Bridge the market stalls are well worth a diversion. *On the San Marco side of the bridge, follow the* fondamenta *along the Grand Canal until you reach Calle del Carbon. Turn left here for Campo San Luca, then right for Campo Manin.*

4 Campo Manin

In a city of beautiful old buildings, the modern Cassa di Risparmio stands out like a sore thumb. Daniele Manin, who led the Venetian uprising against the Austrians in 1848, stands, commemorated as a statue, with his back to the bank, looking towards his house. *Take the tiny street left off the campo, marked Scala Contarini del Bovolo, and follow the signs to a little courtyard.*

5 Scala Contarini del Bovolo

Overlooking a small, secluded courtyard is the prettiest stairway in Venice. In dialect, *bovolo* means 'snail shell', which

describes the arcaded, spiral stairway of the 15th-century Renaissance Palazzo Contarini del Bovol (*Tel: 041 260 1974. www.scaladelbovolo.org. Currently closed for restoration*).
Retrace your steps to Campo Manin and turn left, following the narrow streets to Campo Sant'Angelo. Cross the square to reach Campo Santo Stefano.

6 Campo Santo Stefano

Bullfights and carnival festivities used to take place in this large square. The last bullfight was held here in 1802 when several of the spectators were killed by a falling stand. Café Paolin, near the Gothic Church of Santo Stefano (*see pp58–9*), is a good stop for a coffee or ice cream.

The statue in the centre of the square is of scholar Nicolò Tommaseo, one of the leaders of the anti-Austrian rebellion. Music often wafts from the windows of Palazzo Pisani, which is now the Conservatory of Music, at the far end of the square. This huge palace stands on its own *campo* and fronts on to the Grand Canal.
From the square, take Calle del Spezier, marked to San Marco. It soon traverses Campo San Maurizio where the old church now houses a fascinating collection of ancient musical instruments (free entrance).
This is the main route back to Piazza San Marco, so just follow the flow and, if necessary, the 'San Marco' signs.

Walk: San Marco

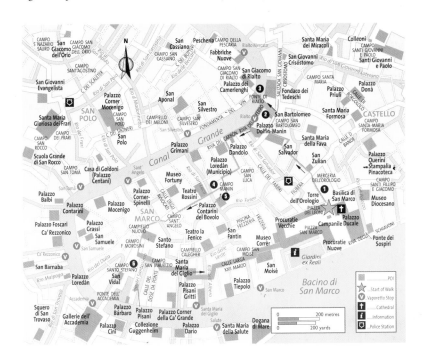

meaning house. Only the fabulous Palazzo Ducale (Doge's Palace) was entitled to be called a *palazzo*.

The architectural masterpieces flanking the canal span some 500 years. The oldest palaces show the influence of the Byzantine style and, as early as the 13th century, the basic design of the Venetian house had been established.

Delicate beauty and domestic comfort came before strict architectural protocol. The house was built on stone slabs, laid over wood, which in turn was supported by hundreds of wooden piles driven into the mud. At water level there was a porticoed entrance to the canal (many such entrances still exist) and ample warehousing space.

A formal stairway led to the first floor (*piano nobile*), on which was a large room used for banquets, balls and other special occasions. This stretched the entire length of the building and afforded fine views of the Grand Canal. In later houses, a second floor, with another balcony over the canal, was used mainly for family bedrooms, and the top floor reserved for servants.

Nowadays, relatively few Venetians have the pleasure of owning an entire *palazzo* on the Grand Canal. Many of the old aristocratic families have disappeared. Today, a considerable number of the buildings are used as offices, hotels and museums, or divided into apartments to be rented out. If a palace or part of a palace is sold, chances are the buyer will be a foreigner or a non-Venetian Italian.

Some of these are bought merely as a *pied-à-terre* and thus remain empty for the greater part of the year.

Four bridges span the canal: the Scalzi, the Rialto, the Accademia and the new Ponte della Costituzione. All four, especially the Rialto and the Accademia, afford fine views of the canal. However, most of the canal itself is inaccessible to pedestrians, who can access only the occasional short quayside from which to view the scene. The best way of seeing the palaces is to board a No 1 *vaporetto*, which travels the entire length of the canal (*see* the Grand Canal boat tour, *pp90–91*). The No 2 covers the same journey, but makes fewer stops.

Alternatively, of course, you could splash out on a gondola or a water-taxi.

Museo Correr

This is a huge museum of history and art, contained within some 70 rooms of the Procuratie Vecchie and the Ala Napoleonica. It is divided into two main sections: history on the first floor and picture gallery on the second floor. Two distinct advantages are the absence of crowds (most tourists sacrifice the Correr in favour of the more famous sights of the Piazza) and the excellent explanations in English throughout.

History section

The major part of the collection commemorates the life and history of the Venetian Republic from its earliest days to its fall in 1797. Notable exceptions are the neoclassical rooms which contain early, naturalistic works by the influential Venetian sculptor Antonio Canova (1757–1822). The variety of historical exhibits, forming what could be described as a fossilised pageant of the Republic, includes prints, paintings, sculpture, coins, medals, books, furniture, costumes and military paraphernalia and armour.

A number of rooms are devoted to the institution of the doge, including depictions of state ceremonies, relics of the Bucintoro (the state barge) and a cap worn by a 15th-century doge. Among the historical themes that are highlighted are Venetian trade with the Orient, the Arsenale and the Battle of Lepanto in 1571 when Venetian and other Christian ships won a resounding victory over the Turks.

Also on the first floor are the Archaeological Museum (*see p55*) and Libreria Sansoviniana (*see pp51 & 54*), which can be visited on the same ticket.

Pinacoteca (Picture gallery)

The collection, second only to that of the Accademia Gallery in Venice, is a superb survey of the evolution of style in Venetian painting, from its earliest times to the beginning of the 16th century. The collection starts with the very earliest pieces of Venetian panel paintings, then progresses through Veneto-Byzantine art to the Gothic, the International Gothic, and finally the Renaissance.

(*Cont. on p42*)

History and art come together in the displays in the Museo Correr

Of gondolas and gondoliers

Four centuries ago the gondola was part of workaday Venice, as common then as the *vaporetto* is today. Of the 10,000 gondolas in the city, 4,000 or so were hired out; the rest were privately owned and used for both business and pleasure. Venetian prostitutes frequently plied their trade from the flat-bottomed craft, and with the development of the *felze*, an intimate little cabin giving total privacy, the gondola became something close to a floating brothel.

The 'shelter of sweet sins' was not the only distinguishing feature of the ancient gondola. The rivalry of nobles was manifest in gondolas that were exotically carved and decorated, and padded with cushions of satin and silk. Sumptuary laws were passed in an effort to curb the excesses, and an edict of 1562 forbade any colouring whatsoever. It was many years, however, before the exotic decoration finally gave way to funereal black.

By the latter half of the 19th century, the gondola's cosy monopoly on transport in Venice had come to an end. In 1881, a French company introduced the *vaporetto*. The 'little

A gondola ride through Venice may leave you with empty pockets, but can't be beaten for viewing the city in traditional, historic style

The gondola, symbol of Venice, has been carrying passengers for over a thousand years

steamer' (or 'screeching kettle' as Ruskin called it) was smoky, noisy and intrusive, but no one could deny it was faster and cheaper than the gondola. Since then, the story of the gondoliers has been largely one of a losing battle. During the last century, they have blockaded the Grand Canal, threatened to burn their gondolas and stormed the town hall, all in an effort to draw public attention to their plight. Meanwhile, the prices steadily rise and the cost of an hour's ride in the evening is now the equivalent of roughly 30 trips in a *vaporetto* round the entire periphery of Venice.

It is not just the notorious greed of the gondoliers that makes for the high prices. The complex construction of the gondola – 280 pieces of timber, cut from nine different types of wood – combined with the regular scraping, tarring and overhauling that is necessary to keep them canal-worthy accounts for a large portion of the cost. Venetians take gondolas only for weddings and funerals, and tourists think twice before paying an arm and a leg. But though the trade is dwindling, Venice is unlikely to let the gondola sink. It is, after all, symbolic of Venice, loved by all who see the city – and even by those who don't.

The great strength of the collection is the range of 15th-century paintings, showing the fusion of Paduan, Ferrarese, Flemish and Tuscan elements to forge the Venetian late 15th-century style. Of particular note are the works of the Ferrarese Cosimo Turà (notably his *Pietà*), Bartolomeo Vivarini, who trained at Padua, the two Flemish painters, Van de Goes and Bouts, and Antonello da Messina, the Sicilian who made a significant impression on a number of young Venetian artists when he visited the city.

The melting pot of these non-Venetian influences is clearly visible in four distinguished works by Giovanni Bellini: the *Pietà*, *Madonna and Child*, the *Transfiguration* and the *Crucifixion*.

The best-known 16th-century paintings in the gallery are the two Carpaccios: *Portrait of a Young Man in a Red Hat* and *Two Courtesans*. The latter title is still generally used, though the consensus of opinion is that the two female figures are probably two bored and respectable bourgeois women sitting with their pets on the patio of their *palazzo*. An over-ecstatic Ruskin once described it as 'the best picture in the world'.

Procuratie Vecchie and Ala Napoleonica, Piazza San Marco, San Marco. Tel: 041 240 5211. www.museicivici veneziani.it. Open: Apr–Oct daily 10am–7pm; Nov–Mar daily 10am–5pm. Admission charge (combined city museums ticket). Vaporetto: any line to San Marco or San Zaccaria.

Museo Fortuny

In the early 20th century, the splendid Gothic Palazzo Pesaro degli Orfei became the home of Mariano Fortuny, the eccentric Spanish painter, sculptor, photographer, stage designer and creator of Fortuny silks. On the death of his widow in 1956, the palace and its contents were bequeathed to the city as a venue for the arts. Exhibits include paintings by Fortuny, the famous pleated silk Fortuny dresses and Fortuny textiles. Temporary art exhibitions are held here.

Palazzo Pesaro degli Orfei, Campo San Beneto, San Marco. Tel: 041 520 0995. Currently closed for restoration except during exhibitions (Wed–Mon 10am–6pm). Admission charge. Vaporetto: No 1 to Sant'Angelo.

Palazzo Ducale (Doge's Palace)

All the history of Venice, all its splendid stately past, glows around you in a strong sea-light.

Henry James, *Italian Hours*, 1899.

FORTUNY

Mariano Fortuny y Madrazo, or Don Mariano, as he loved to be called, was born in Granada in 1871. He came to Venice in his 30s and spent the rest of his life in Palazzo Pesaro degli Orfei, painting, sculpting, designing textiles and developing new ideas on scenography. He reintroduced the ancient Venetian techniques of weaving cloth with threads of gold and silver and also re-created dyes used in the 16th century. His fabrics, and particularly the pleated Fortuny silk dresses, became the rage in the early 20th century.

The Scala dei Giganti leads into the Doge's Palace

Home of the doge and seat of the government and law courts, Palazzo Ducale was the powerhouse of the Venetian Republic. The interior, whose huge rooms are decorated with dimly lit, monumental paintings, lacks the light and airy quality of its pink, shimmering façade. The furniture was wrecked or pillaged by Napoleon and the original 14th- and 15th-century works of art destroyed by various fires.

What you see today is the palace of the 16th century, the walls and ceilings decorated with works by the leading painters of the time. The emphasis is on the history and glorification of the Republic through mythological themes, allegories and huge depictions of historical events.

Recent projects include the conservation of the original 14th-century capitals (in the Museo dell'Opera) and the reopening of a ground-floor wing which displays archaeological features and sculptures. Restoration is constantly under way, so don't be surprised if at least one section of the palace is closed.

Having entered from the lagoon quayside, visitors then walk across the courtyard, off which you will find an atmospheric café.

Anticollegio

The waiting room for ambassadors and dignitaries, this has some of the finest paintings in the palace, including four mythological scenes by Tintoretto and ceiling paintings by Veronese. The finest work is Veronese's radiant *Rape of Europe*, facing the window wall.

Arco Foscari/Scala dei Giganti

The vaulted passageway leads to the Arco Foscari, decorated on the far side by bronze figures of *Adam* and *Eve* –

copies of the marble originals inside the palace. The portico leads to the Scala dei Giganti (Giants' Stairway), the giants being Sansovino's *Neptune* and *Mars*, whose monumental and somewhat incongruous figures stand at the top of this splendid staircase.

From 1485 the doges were crowned here. The lovely Renaissance courtyard has two fine bronze wellheads. The public formerly had free access here to take drinking water or shelter under the arcades.

Itinerari Segreti (Secret Itinerary)

This is the tour to take if you want to see the parts of the palace that are normally kept under lock and key. These include the rooms and hall of the chancellery, interrogation chambers, the torture chamber and the *piombi* (dungeons). The 90-minute tour is comprehensive and informative.

Porta della Cartà

Squeezed between the side of the Basilica and the corner of the palace, this gateway is now the exit. The origin of the name probably stems from either the nearby *cartae* (archives) or the notices that used to be posted here. The ornate gate was carved in florid Gothic style between 1438 and 1443 by Bartolomeo and Giovanni Bon for Doge Foscari, who is seen kneeling in front of the Lion of San Marco. This marble group is a 19th-century replica of the original, which was destroyed by Napoleon.

Prigioni (Prisons)/Ponte dei Sospiri (Bridge of Sighs)

The palace was specially designed so that prisoners could be whisked away from the council rooms of the Doge's Palace across the Ponte dei Sospiri – the Bridge of Sighs, so named because of the lamentation of the condemned who crossed the bridge on their way to the dungeons on the other side. However, the bridge was not constructed until 1600, by which time the prisons were, by European standards, quite tolerable and reserved for minor offenders only.

The *pozzi* (wells), on the lower two storeys, were the grimmest of the dungeons: dark, dank and rat-infested. Lesser criminals were kept in the *piombi*, and it was from these prisons that the famous libertine, Casanova masterminded his dramatic escape. According to Casanova, prisons were salubrious, with plenty to eat, comfortable beds, and clothes and clean laundry when you needed it.

Sala d'Armi (Armoury)

Despite dispersal of the armoury after the Fall of the Republic, this is still a rich collection. The prize piece is the suit of armour of King Henry IV of France, who presented it to the city in 1603.

Sala del Collegio

It was here that the doge gathered with his Council of State. The room has a splendid carved and gilded ceiling with allegorical figures by Veronese and, notably, an outstanding depiction of

Justice and Peace Offering the Sword and Scales to Venice Enthroned, in the centre of the far end.

Sala del Consiglio dei Dieci/ Sala della Bussola

The Consiglio dei Dieci, or Council of Ten, was a powerful body elected to oversee the security of the state. A sort of secret service, the group was chosen by the Senate for one year, but members' names were never divulged. One of their duties was to observe the movements of the doge and the senators.

The finest works of art in the room are two ceiling paintings by Veronese: *Juno Offering Venice the Doge's Cap* and *An Old Oriental Man with a Young Woman*.

The following Sala della Bussola was the waiting room for the accused and witnesses about to appear before the Council of Ten. The *bocca di leone* (lion's mouth), near the door, served as the postbox for secret denunciations.

Sala del Maggior Consiglio

Impressive for sheer size alone, this assembly hall accommodated 3,000 guests when Henry III of France was entertained here at a state banquet in 1574. It was here that the doge and other members of government were elected by the 480 members of the Maggior Consiglio, later to extend their number to 1,700.

Tintoretto's monumental *Paradise*, inspired by Dante, covers the eastern wall. Measuring 22m by 7m (72ft by

23ft), it is the largest Old Master oil painting in the world. The carved and gilded wooden ceiling is panelled with scenes celebrating Venice, and painted by leading artists of the time, including Tintoretto and Veronese, whose *Apotheosis* stands out for its dramatic perspective. The frieze of portraits around the room depicts the first 76 doges, with the exception of one. The space with a black veil should belong to Marin Falier, the doge executed for treason in 1355.

Sala delle Quattro Porte

Named after its four Palladian portals, the room is decorated with a lavish white and gilt stucco ceiling with paintings by Tintoretto. The wall painting of *Doge Grimani Adoring Faith*, on the right of the entrance, was begun by Titian and (*Cont. on p48*)

The iconic Bridge of Sighs

The doge: last among equals

Doges are not gentlemen, not even Dukes, but the glorified slaves of the Republic.

Petrarch (after the execution of Doge Falier)

The doge was arguably Europe's first constitutional monarch. Tradition has it that Paoluccio Anafesto was the first doge, appointed by the Byzantium Empire in 697. The rest were elected by an aristocratic oligarchy, and they held the post for life. In the early days, the doge was the supreme authority, but as the republican constitution developed, his powers and privileges diminished. The Great Council was set up in the late 12th century as a kind of permanent oligarchy which took the weightiest decisions of state, such as appointing ministers and declaring war.

By the end of the 14th century, the constitution fettered the liberty of the doge in ways which might surprise even a monarch today. He could not answer questions on foreign policy without consulting his councillors, nor entertain a foreign visitor in private, nor leave the city without the express

Detail of the Doge's Palace

View of the Palace from St Mark's Basin

permission of the Great Council. His income was strictly controlled, his mail scrutinised by censors, and the only gifts he could accept were flowers and herbs.

Some doges, such as Foscari, who instigated vast mainland conquests, or Dandolo, who masterminded the Fourth Crusade, did manage to influence policy. But Doge Falier, who attempted to hijack the constitution, was promptly executed for conspiracy.

While the powers of the doge were curtailed, the ceremonies surrounding his election and death lost none of their splendour. On Coronation Day, the doge and his entourage were transported in the gilt state barge to Palazzo Ducale, to be crowned with regal pomp at the top of the Scala dei Giganti. On his death, the palace was closed, and the body carried ceremoniously around the Piazza prior to the funeral service in San Marco.

probably completed by his workshop. The easel painting is *Venice Receiving the Homage of Neptune* by G B Tiepolo.

Sala del Senato

This was the room where the doge met with members of the Senate to discuss domestic and foreign issues. The centrepiece of the ornate ceiling is Tintoretto's *Triumph of Venice*, the figure of Venice set high in the clouds, surrounded by the gods of Olympus. Hanging over the throne, *The Dead Christ Worshipped by Doges Pietro Lando and Marcantonio Trevisan* is by the same artist.

Scala d'Oro/Private Apartments

Leading to the doge's apartments, this sumptuously decorated staircase was built between 1538 and 1559. The gold stucco gave it the name of the Golden Staircase. The Sala degli Scarlatti (first of the apartments) has the finest features, with an original gilded wooden ceiling, a fireplace sculpted by Antonio and Tullio Lombardo, and a finely carved marble relief by Pietro Lombardo above the doors. At the top of the Scala d'Oro, the square vestibule has a 16th-century gilded wooden ceiling with Tintoretto's painting of *Justice and Peace Offering the Sword and Scales to the Doge* (1559–67).

Piazzetta San Marco. Tel: 041 271 5911. www.museiciviciveneziani.it. Open: Apr–Oct daily 8.30am–6.30pm; Nov–Mar daily 8.30am–5.30pm. Ticket office shuts 1 hour before closing time. The 'Secret Itinerary' guided tour takes place in English three times a day (at 9.55am, 10.45am & 11.35am) and must be booked in advance. Tel: 041 520 9070.

Palazzo Grassi – now an exhibition centre thanks to corporate interest in the city's heritage

Admission charge (combined with city museums ticket). Vaporetto: any to San Marco or San Zaccaria.

Palazzo Grassi

The most exciting contemporary art gallery in Venice, this neoclassical *palazzo* on the Grand Canal was designed by Giorgio Massari in 1749 around a large colonnaded courtyard. It was one of the last palaces built before the fall of the Venetian Republic. Bought by the Fiat group, under Gianni Agnelli, in 1983, it was used as an exhibition space for several years, but closed down in 2005 after Agnelli's death. It was then bought by French luxury goods tycoon François Pinault in conjunction with the city-owned Casinò Municipale di Venezia. The owners hired Japanese architect Tadao Ando to remodel the interior prior to its reopening in April 2006. Pinault owns a vast collection (over 2,000 works) of modern art, and the gallery mounts themed shows based on his collection, as well as specially commissioned works. The *palazzo* has a good café, serving simple salads and pastas, managed by the well-known Vecio Fritolin restaurant. The art on the wall of the café changes according to the main exhibition. Last entrance an hour before closing. Check the website for exhibition details.

Campo San Samuele, San Marco. Tel: 041 199 139 139 (from Italy) or 0039 0445 230 313 (Ticket Office). www.palazzograssi.it. Open: Wed–Mon

The omnipresent winged lion of St Mark

10am–7pm. Admission charge. It is possible to buy a joint ticket for Palazzo Grassi and Punta della Dogana (see p82).

Piazza San Marco (St Mark's Square)

More praise has been heaped on Piazza San Marco than on any other square in the world. It is not only the architecture which inspires – though the blend of exotic East and classical West is naturally one of its most intriguing aspects – it is also the fact that this is, and has been for centuries, the very heart and soul of the city. Over the centuries it has seen bullfights and pig hunts, pageants and processions, feast days, carnivals and a host of other spectacular events. Modern festivities may be tame by comparison, but the square is still a splendid stage setting which, while fleecing you of your last euro, continues to captivate and enchant.

Commercialism and tourism in the Piazza are nothing new. Foreign merchants used to gather here, and travellers have always been lured by its charms. In 1751, John Moore, an English visitor to Venice, wrote of the melting pot of characters seen in the square in the early evening: 'a mixed multitude of Jews, Turks and Christians; lawyers, knaves and pickpockets; mountebanks, old women and physicians; women of quality, with masks; strumpets barefaced; and, in short, such a jumble of senators, citizens, gondoliers and people of every character and condition.' Moneylenders set up kiosks here, vendors sold wine and street artists entertained, while the rich and fashionable looked on from the *piazza* cafés.

Nowadays, the Piazza swarms with tourists for most months of the year. Mingling among them are portrait artists, souvenir sellers, pigeon seed vendors, Murano glass factory touts and multilingual tour guides.

Happily, Venetians still come here, either for coffee or a drink at Florian's, or an evening stroll or *passeggiata*. All day the square is a scene of constant activity and one that rarely fails to entertain. Only in midwinter, when the mists roll in from the lagoon and the square is splashed by high tides, does it assume a more melancholy air.

Campanile

For centuries the *campanile*, or bell tower, of San Marco was used as a watchtower and a lighthouse for vessels entering the lagoon. Work on the first tower started in the late 9th century,

ST MARK AND THE LION

It is difficult to go far in Venice without encountering the winged lion of St Mark. There are around 2,000 in the city and hundreds more in the Veneto. In a number of sculptures, the lion's paw is clamped on the open pages of a book by the inscription *Pax tibi Marce, Evangelista meus* (Peace to you Mark, my Evangelist). Legend has it that these were the words of an angel who appeared to St Mark in a dream. Following the fall of the Venetian Republic, Napoleon destroyed hundreds of the carved lions but many of these were replaced by 19th-century reproductions.

but was not complete until 1173. Following an earthquake in the early 16th century, it was heavily restored and the golden angel, forming a weathervane, was ceremoniously positioned on the top.

The tower had five bells, each of which had a different role. The largest, called the Marangona, summoned people to work early in the morning, then tolled again at breakfast time. In the Middle Ages, the tower was used to support a torture cage where hapless offenders were left dangling for days.

On 14 July 1902, the 98.6m (323ft)-tall *campanile* came crashing down and over 10,000 tonnes of bricks and marble lay in a great heap where the tower had stood. The cause was a combination of past earthquakes, lightning and general wear and tear. Miraculously, the basilica and library escaped unscathed. It was Sansovino's *loggetta*, at the foot of the tower, that bore the brunt of the fall; but the

San Marco – the most famous *piazza* in Venice

structure was painstakingly rebuilt using the pieces of debris.

The foundation stone for the new tower was laid less than a year after its collapse. It was agreed that the tower should be rebuilt exactly as it was before and on precisely the same spot.

To see what a 16th-century English traveller once described as 'the fairest and goodliest prospect that is (I thinke) in all the world', take the lift up to the bell chamber. From here, there are wonderful views of the city, the islands and, on a clear day, the snowy peaks of the Alps. You can see why Galileo used this spot in 1609 to demonstrate his telescope to the doge. Interestingly enough, the canals of the city are not visible from this high viewpoint – only the tightly packed buildings, the towers and the spires.

At the base of the *campanile*, a plaque indicates the water level which was reached during the catastrophic floods of 4 November 1966.

Campanile tel: 041 270 8311. www. basilicasanmarco.it. Open: Nov–Easter daily 9.30am–3.45pm; Easter–Jun & Oct daily 9am–7pm; Jul–Sept daily 9am–9pm. Admission charge.

Libreria Sansoviniana

Opposite the Doge's Palace, the library is the masterpiece of Jacopo Sansovino. Built between 1537 and 1588, it was described by the 16th-century architect Andrea Palladio as the most ornate and beautiful building since antiquity. With its Doric and Ionic orders, its swags and sculptures, and the play of light in its colonnades, the building was a model

(*Cont. on p54*)

Walk: Piazzale to Piazza

This route weaves through the heart of Venice, taking you from one hub of the city (Piazzale Roma) to another (Piazza San Marco).

Allow 2 hours, excluding sightseeing.

Starting at Piazzale Roma, cross Rio Nuovo, walk past the gardens and cross the canal beyond.

1 San Nicolò da Tolentino

Construction work on this huge church with a striking Corinthian porch began in 1590, but it was not completed until the 18th century. The cannonball lodged in the wall was left by the Austrians in 1849. Sculptures and paintings decorate the church's interior. *Return to the bridge and follow the signs for San Giovanni Evangelista and the Dentro Venezia itinerary.*

2 San Giovanni Evangelista

The highlight of this complex of Scuola, square and church is the elegant entrance on the far side. Go through the archway and look back to see Pietro Lombardo's beautifully carved marble portal. The Scuola has a splendid double staircase by Coducci and a sumptuous main hall. (For admission to the Scuola, telephone in advance *041 718 234*.)

Beyond the portal, turn right and first left. Cross Campo San Stin and the bridge on the far side.

3 Campo dei Frari

The monumental façade of the Frari now faces you. The finest of the doorway bas-reliefs is the 15th-century Tuscan carving of the *Madonna and Child with Angels*, on the north side. Nothing, however, prepares you for the majesty of the interior (*see p63*) and its works of art. Another rich repository of art is the neighbouring Scuola Grande di San Rocco (*see pp71–2*).
From the south side of the square, follow the Rialto signs to Campo San Tomà.

4 Campo San Tomà

This is a pretty square with a *trattoria* and silver shops. At this end the Scuola dei Calerghieri (shoemakers) has a delightful relief of *St Mark Healing the Cobbler Ananias*, by Pietro Lombardo. *Follow the 'Traghetto' sign at the far end of the square.*

5 Traghetto

A *traghetto* is the cheapest way of travelling by gondola. Venetians stand for the crossing as the two gondoliers deftly weave through the traffic, while the less trusting tourists tend to grab a seat.

On the far side, the narrow street ahead leads into the Piscina San Samuele. At the end turn left for Campo Santo Stefano (see p37). Turn left again to reach Campo Sant'Angelo and take the first right turn off the square (Calle Caotorta). Cross the bridge and turn left over a second bridge.

6 Teatro la Fenice

The ornate interior of the 18th-century Fenice theatre, 'Jewel of Italian Opera', was devoured by flames in January 1996. This was the third fire to destroy the opera house (*see p158*). Funds poured in for its reconstruction, which was completed in 2004.

The sottoportego (alley) beyond brings you round to the front of the Fenice and into Campo San Fantin.

The street on the left of San Fantin Church becomes the Frezzeria.

7 Frezzeria

In medieval times, this was the main street for buying *freccie* (arrows). Later, the alley acquired a reputation for prostitution. Nowadays, it is a busy, narrow shopping street, lined by exotic and off-beat boutiques.

At the end of the Frezzeria, turn left for Piazza San Marco.

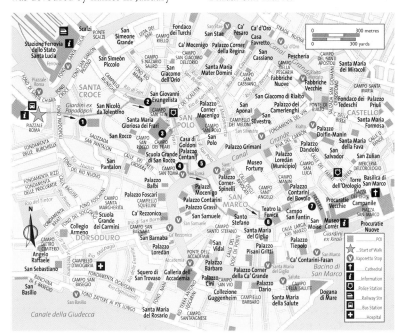

Feeding the pigeons – a one-time daily ritual in St Mark's Square

for the High Renaissance which Sansovino brought to Venice.

During the construction of the library in 1545, a severe frost caused the ceiling of the Great Hall to collapse. The unfortunate Sansovino was blamed for the disaster and put in prison. Only through the persuasive powers of friends in high places, Titian among them, was his release granted.

The library has a splendid stuccoed stairway, fully restored, and a main hall with painted ceiling medallions by Veronese and other artists. Other treasures are a fascinating map of the world drawn by Fra Mauro in the 15th century and Marco Polo's will. *Entry via Museo Correr (see pp38–9 & 42). Tel: 041 520 8788. Open: Apr–Oct daily 9am–7pm; Nov–Mar daily 9am–5pm. Free guided tours on Sundays (for information and bookings, contact mazzariol@marciana.venezia.sbn.it).*

Loggetta

At the foot of the *campanile*, the elegant marble *loggetta* was designed by Sansovino in the form of a triumphal arch. It was built as a *ridotto dei nobili* (meeting place for the nobles), taking the place of the wooden stalls that used to stand here. In 1569 it became a guardroom for the *arsenalotti* (arsenal workers), then in the 18th century it

PIGEONS

The pigeons are an integral part of *piazza* life, perching and defecating on every available statue, eroding the stone and contributing to Venice's perennial problems of pollution. A scheme to eradicate birdlife from the square by introducing birth control seed was shortlived; however, a more long-term plan has seen birdfood sellers ejected from the square and has made it illegal to feed the pigeons. Nevertheless, these birds have delighted young and old here for centuries.

was used as the headquarters of the city's lottery.

Rebuilt after the collapse of the *campanile* in 1902, the *loggetta* is richly decorated with reliefs and has bronze allegorical statues by Sansovino – *Pallas*, *Apollo*, *Mercury* and *Peace* – all representing virtues to which the government aspired. Inside the *loggetta*, where tourists queue for the lift to the top of the tower, you can see Sansovino's reconstructed terracotta of *The Madonna and Child with St John*.

Museo Archeologico (Museum of Archaeology)

Adjoining the Sansoviniana Library, this museum houses an extensive collection of Greek and Roman sculpture. Since it is upstaged by the more famous sights of the Piazza, the museum is undeservedly quiet and empty. The collection, which had a marked influence on Venetian painters and sculptors, was bequeathed to the state by Cardinal Domenico Grimani, son of Doge Antonio Grimani.
Entry via Museo Correr (see pp38–9 & 42). Tel: 041 522 5978. www.museicivici veneziani.it. Open: daily 8.15am– 7.15pm. Admission charge.

Piazzetta

Flanked by the Doge's Palace and the Libreria Sansoviniana, the area called the Piazzetta was originally a harbour. In the 12th century it was filled in and the two lofty red and grey granite columns, looted from the Orient, were erected on the stretch near the waterfront, called the Molo. One is surmounted by the winged lion of St Mark, the other by a statue of the former patron saint of the city, St Theodore, armed with shield and standing on a dragon (which looks like a crocodile). A third column fell into the lagoon and was never recovered.

Nicolò Barattieri, the engineer who achieved the remarkable feat of erecting the two columns, was said to have been rewarded with the gambling monopoly in Venice, the proviso being that the gaming tables were set between the two columns. Up until 1753, this was also the venue for public executions.

In the early 17th century, the English writer Thomas Coryat spoke of the

The Torre dell'Orologio bell strikes on the hour

stench of the heads of enemies or traitors of the state being laid out here for three days and nights.

Procuratie

The Procuratie Vecchie are the 16th-century arcaded buildings on the left of the square as you look towards the basilica. These were built to house the Procuratie, or high-ranking officials of the old republic, and were then rebuilt in the 16th century, aggrandised and enlarged with an upper storey. To balance these, the Procuratie Nuove were built in the 16th to 17th centuries.

The two Procuratie are joined by the Ala Napoleonica, named after Napoleon who, despite his quote about the Piazza being 'the most elegant drawing room in Europe', knocked down the Church of San Geminiano and built a new arcade with a ballroom above.

Torre dell'Orologio (Clock Tower)

Recently renovated, the clock tower (1496–9) at one end of the Procuratie Vecchie, above an archway to the Mercerie, was begun by the Venetian Renaissance architect Mauro Coducci. The clock, with its gold and enamel face, shows not only the time but the phases of the moon and movement of the sun in relation to zodiac signs. To see the full works of the tower, you should be in Venice during Ascension week (in May), when the Magi, preceded by an Angel, appear from a side door, as the clock strikes the hour, and bow before a figure of the Virgin and Child. On the upper section of the tower, the symbolic Lion of St Mark is set against a blue background with gold stars. At the top, two giant bronze figures strike the hour. These are known as 'The Moors' because of their dark patina. There are guided tours in English. Note that they aren't recommended for those with walking or breathing difficulties.
Bookings on 041 4273 0892. Mon–Wed 10am & 11am; Thur–Sun 2pm & 3pm.

Zecca (Mint)

Another triumph of architecture by Sansovino, this was built between 1537 and 1545 on the site of the former mint. The Zecca gave its name to the Zecchino, or Venetian ducat.
On the Piazzetta, overlooking the waterfront and adjoining the Libreria Sansoviniana.

San Giuliano/San Zulian

In the midst of the bustling Mercerie is San Giuliano, a richly decorated church rebuilt in the 16th century and financed by philosopher and physician Tommaso Rangone, whose bronze statue by Sansovino stands above the door. More evidence of self-glorification are the inscriptions and carvings on the façade, showing Rangone's genius as a scholar.
Campo San Zulian, San Marco. Tel: 041 523 5383. Open: daily 8.30am–7pm (Mass in English daily 11.30am). Vaporetto: any to Rialto or San Marco.

Santa Maria della Fava

Fava in Italian means 'bean'; the church was named after the bean-shaped *dolci* (sweet biscuits) sold in a local *pasticceria* (cake shop) on All Souls' Day. Architecturally the church is unremarkable, but there are two altarpieces that make it worthy of a visit: Piazzetta's *Virgin and St Philip Neri* (1725–7), second altar on the left, and Tiepolo's *Education of the Virgin* (1732), first altar on the right, an early work showing how the artist was beginning to break free from the influence of Piazzetta's sombre canvases.

Campo Santa Maria della Fava, San Marco. Tel: 041 522 4601. Open: Mon–Sat 8.30am–noon & 4.30–7pm, Sun 8.30am–noon. Vaporetto: Nos 1 & 2 to Rialto.

JACOPO SANSOVINO (1486–1570)

Jacopo Tatti was born in Florence and trained under Andrea Sansovino, whose name he adopted. In the early 16th century, he was working in Rome sculpting and restoring statues. In 1527, he fled from the Sack of Rome, stopping at Venice on his way to France. However, a commission to restore the main cupola of San Marco led to his appointment as Chief Architect of the Republic and he stayed in Venice for the rest of his life.

In addition to the library, the mint and the *loggetta*, Sansovino designed several Venetian palaces, the churches of San Giuliano and San Francesco della Vigna (which was completed by Palladio), and the statues of *Neptune* and *Mars* on the ceremonial staircase in the Doge's Palace. His buildings, designed on ancient Roman structures, epitomised the High Renaissance in Venice.

Santa Maria del Giglio (or Zobenigo)

The Baroque façade of the Giglio church was financed by the Barbaro family and erected between 1678 and 1683. It was built not to the glory of God – there is a noticeable absence of religious images – but to the glory of the male members of the Barbaro family and their militaristic pursuits. Statues of the brothers are surrounded by trophies, vessels and war memorabilia, while further down a series of relief carvings shows the cities of Zara, Candia, Padua, Rome, Corfu and Split – all places connected with Antonio Barbaro's naval and diplomatic career.

The wealth of paintings inside the church includes *The Madonna and Child with the Young St John*, attributed to Rubens, and two paintings of the evangelists by Tintoretto. These hang in the sanctuary.

Campo Santa Maria del Giglio, San Marco. Tel: 041 275 0462. www. chorusvenezia.org. Open: Mon–Sat 10am–5pm. Admission charge. Vaporetto: No 1 to Santa Maria del Giglio.

San Moisè

John Ruskin considered San Moisè the most 'clumsy' church in Venice, 'illustrative of the last degradation of the Renaissance'. The façade, one of the most conspicuous in Venice, is covered in confusing clusters of Baroque carvings. Depending on your taste, this may be more acceptable than the stark modern façade of the Bauer Grünwald flanking the same square.

Predictably, the interior has an elaboration of period paintings and sculpture. The most eye-catching, but hardly the most beautiful, feature is the high altar representing *Moses on Mount Sinai Receiving the Tablets*. From a distance this looks more like a watersplashed rockery.

Campo San Moisè, San Marco. Tel: 041 270 2464. Open: Mon–Sat 9.30am–12.30pm. Vaporetto: any to San Marco.

San Salvador

The large church of San Salvador lies on the well-trodden route between Piazza San Marco and the Rialto, its frequently used back entrance squeezed between a couple of shops. The spacious Renaissance interior – created by the combined inspiration of Sparento, Tullio Lombardo and Sansovino – houses important works of art, including two paintings by Titian. One of these is an *Annunciation* (third altar on the right), painted when the artist was in his 80s.

Under a restoration project funded by the American Save Venice Organization, centuries of dirt and varnish were removed, to reveal a riot of colour and light, painted with the dramatic, impressionistic brushstrokes which typify Titian's later works. Above the high altar is another late Titian, the *Transfiguration of Christ*. On festivals and special occasions this is lowered

Santo Stefano's 16th-century *campanile* has a distinct tilt

into the crypt by an ingenious device to reveal a splendid silver-gilt reredos.

Campo San Salvador, San Marco. Tel: 041 523 6717. www.chiesasan salvador.it. Open: Apr–Oct Mon–Sat 9am–noon & 4–6.30pm, Sun 4–7pm; Nov–Mar Mon–Sat 9am–noon & 3–6.30pm, Sun 3–7pm. Vaporetto: Nos 1 & 2 to Rialto.

Santo Stefano

Lying at the northern end of Campo Santo Stefano is this fine Gothic church with a leaning *campanile*. The original church was built for the Hermits of St Augustine in the 14th century, then radically altered, and completed in the 15th century. The upper section of the 60m (197ft)-high tower collapsed when it was struck by lightning in 1544, and surrounding buildings were damaged. It was rebuilt, and the bells, which came from English churches deconsecrated by Queen Elizabeth I, were recast at the Arsenale.

During the first 250 years of its history, the church was deconsecrated six times for the blood that was shed within its walls. Sitting in its calm interior today, it is hard to believe it ever witnessed scenes of violence.

The church is entered through a fine portal, carved in decorated Gothic style by Bartolomeo Bon. The handsome interior has a long spacious nave and side aisles divided by slender red Verona and Greek marble columns. The splendid ship's-keel roof is decorated with medallions.

The sacristy is the main repository for the works of art. Well lit, if a little grimy, paintings by Jacopo Tintoretto and Bartolomeo Vivarini, among others, grace the walls. The spacious cloisters, now the tax office premises,

can be glimpsed from the bridge leading to Campo Sant'Angelo, nearby.

The Campiello Novo, off Calle del Pestrin and facing the church, was the old burial ground of Santo Stefano. During the plague of 1630, hundreds of corpses were buried here.

Campo Francesco Morosini già Santo Stefano, San Marco. Tel: 041 275 0462. www.chorusvenezia.org. Open: Mon–Sat 10am–5pm. Admission charge to the Sacristy only. Vaporetto: Nos 1 & 2 to Accademia, or No 1 to Sant'Angelo.

San Vidal

The Church of San Vidal is deconsecrated and used for concerts. Still *in situ* in the church is Carpaccio's painting of *San Vitale*, and Sebastiano Ricci's *Immaculate Conception.*

Campo San Vidal, San Marco. Tel: 041 277 0561. Open: daily 9.30am–6pm. Vaporetto: Nos 1 & 2 to Accademia or 2 to San Samuele. Open: during concerts (see p158).

The lofty wooden ceiling of Santo Stefano is one of two in the city that resemble the inverted hull of a ship, the other being San Giacomo dell'Orio in the *sestiere* of Santa Croce (*see p69*)

San Polo and Santa Croce

These neighbouring districts are so closely connected that it is easy to meander unknowingly between the two. San Polo is historically and architecturally more important, with the gargantuan Frari Basilica, the plethora of Tintorettos at the Scuola Grande di San Rocco and the somewhat more prosaic fish market at Rialto. This is not to say that Santa Croce is not also worth visiting: treats include wonderful museums, one of the city's most curious churches, a clutch of excellent restaurants and charming streets and squares.

Campo San Polo

This is the biggest square in Venice after Piazza San Marco. Unlike the more formal square, it lends itself to children's activities such as roller-skating, cycling, and kicking footballs at ancient palaces; this, notwithstanding the stone plaque on the exterior of the apse of the church which threatens prison, galleys, exile and a fine for all games near the church. It is also home to the open-air cinema over the summer months.

The scene today is very different from that of the 18th century, when bullfights, tournaments, masked balls, fairs and festivals were held in the square. On a more gruesome note, in 1546, it witnessed the carefully planned murder of Lorenzino de' Medici who had, nine years earlier, murdered his cousin Alessandro, the Duke of Florence.

One of the finest of the palaces overlooking the *campo* is the pink Gothic **Palazzo Soranzo**. It was here,

playing as a musician at a marriage celebration, that Casanova met the man who was to become his close friend and guardian, Senator Matteo Giovanni Bragadin. The senator offered him a lift home but in the gondola he was struck by apoplexy. Casanova saved his life: he rushed for a surgeon, who bled the dying man, and Bragadin survived. (For the Church of San Polo, see p70, and for Palazzo Corner Mocenigo, see p67.)

Ca' Pesaro

In 1899, the Duchessa Felicità Bevilacqua La Masa bequeathed her grand Baroque Ca' Pesaro to the city on condition that it became a venue for the exhibitions and studios of Italian avant-garde and unknown artists. The year 1902 saw the inauguration of the **Galleria Internazionale d'Arte Moderna** (Museum of Modern Art), which was not quite what the duchess had in mind.

The collection, which was closed for years for restoration, finally reopened in

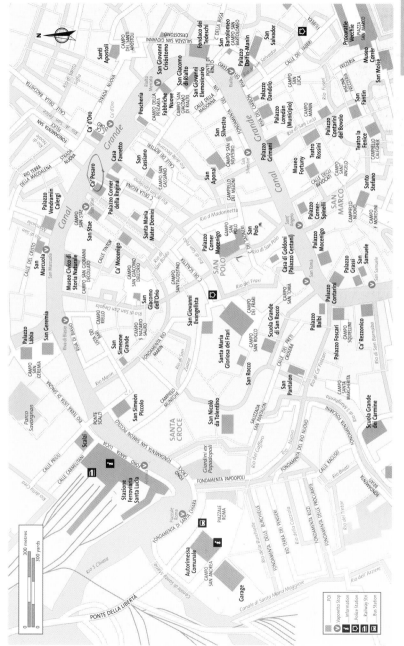

late 2002. The standard is varied, and includes works by very minor Italian artists, as well as those by Kandinsky, Klee, Chagall, Mirò and other internationally renowned modern artists. Temporary exhibitions are occasionally held here. The **Museo d'Arte Orientale** (Museum of Oriental Art) is a very specialised museum, devoted to Japanese art and artefacts collected by the Count of Barbi during his late 19th-century travels in the Far East.

San Stae, Santa Croce. Tel: 04 172 1127. www.museicivicineveneziani.it. Open: Apr–Oct Tue–Sun 10am–6pm; Nov–Mar Tue–Sun 10am–5pm. Closed: Mon.

Admission charge. Vaporetto: No 1 to San Stae.

Frari
(Santa Maria Gloriosa dei Frari)

Founded by the Franciscans, the Frari vies with the Santi Giovanni e Paolo as the greatest Gothic church in Venice. In keeping with the Franciscan principle of poverty, the soaring brick façade is unadorned. The spacious interior, however, has a wealth of paintings, sculpture and tombs, and in this respect the building is as much a gallery as a church – which perhaps explains the fact that sightseers (as opposed to

The Frari's dignified interior is a rich repository of paintings and monuments

worshippers) have to pay to go in. The description below covers only the highlights. For full details, purchase the guidebook sold inside the basilica.

Façade

Although the church was begun in 1330, it was not consecrated until 1492. The only decorations on the façade are the 15th- and 16th-century reliefs, most notably those above the doorways on the north side. The 70m (230ft)-high bell tower is the second highest in Venice after the Campanile of San Marco (*see pp50–51*).

Interior

Keep your entrance ticket, which has a useful, if microscopic, diagram on the back detailing the works of art. The interior is striking for its sheer size. It is built in the form of a Latin Cross, the bays joined by tie beams and the arches supported by 12 hefty columns.

Works of art are spread throughout the church, but the one that will immediately draw your attention is Titian's glorious *Assumption*. This was the artist's first major religious commission, yet it demonstrates his full mastery of colour, composition and light. It was innovative, too, in that the Madonna is no longer shown praying (as some of the friars would have liked) but is depicted floating up towards God the Father.

Apse chapels The first chapel on the right of the chancel contains

Donatello's naturalistic wooden statue of John the Baptist (1450). In the chapel on the far right is Bartolomeo Vivarini's polyptych, *Madonna with Saints* (1482), still in its original frame. The third chapel to the left of the chancel contains the grave of Monteverdi and an altarpiece of *St Ambrose* by Alvise Vivarini and Marco Basaiti. In the Corner Chapel at the end of the left transept is *St Mark Enthroned*, by Bartolomeo Vivarini.

Left aisle A second great work by Titian is on display in the church: the *Pesaro Madonna*, painted eight years after the *Assumption*. This was commissioned by the Pesaro family, members of whom can be seen in the lower right half of the painting. Described by the Swiss historian Jacob Burckhardt as 'a work of quite unfathomable beauty', this again is dynamic in composition and colouring. It was also one of the first works where the Virgin was shown off-centre.

The monument to Antonio Canova, a somewhat incongruous neoclassical marble pyramid, is based on Canova's own design for a monument to Titian that never materialised.

Monks' choir In the centre of the nave, the huge choir consists of 124 beautifully carved stalls. The finest detail is on the upper tier, showing bas-reliefs of saints with Venetian streets, squares and houses on the panels below.

Ca' Pesaro: now an exhibition space for unknown and internationally renowned Italian artists

Right aisle Titian's monument (opposite Canova's) is a ponderous piece of neoclassicism, featuring the artist in the centre with his *Assumption* behind. Titian died of the plague in 1576 and specifically requested to be buried in the Frari. It was the emperor of Austria who met his request, but only 300 years after his death.

Sacristy The highlight here is Giovanni Bellini's *Madonna and Child with Saints* (1488). Henry James sums it up: 'nothing in Venice is more perfect than this … it is as solemn as it is gorgeous and as simple as it is deep.'
Campo dei Frari, San Polo. Tel: 041 275 0462. www.chorusvenezia.org.

Open: Mon–Sat 9am–6pm, Sun 1–6pm. Admission charge. Vaporetto: Nos 1 & 2 to San Tomà.

Museo Civico di Storia Naturale (Natural History Museum)

Once inhabited by Turkish merchants, the building now houses minerals, shells and fossils, and sufficient fish, crustacea and creepy-crawlies to keep any young child entertained. The museum reopened in 2010 after lengthy restoration work and a complete overhaul of its exhibition spaces.

Many of the exhibits, such as the model fishing boats and predecessors of the gondolas, relate to the Venetian lagoon. Others, such as the 11m (36ft)-

long fossil of the *Sarcosuchus imperator* (ancestor of the crocodile), come from further afield.

Fondaco dei Turchi, Canal Grande, Santa Croce. Tel: 041 275 0206. www.museiciviciveneziani.it. Open: Wed 9am–5pm, Sat–Sun 10am–6pm. Admission charge. Vaporetto: No 1 to San Stae.

Palazzo Mocenigo (Ca' Mocenigo)

The 17th-century palace was the home of an aristocratic Venetian family. It retains its 18th-century frescoes and furnishings, and still has the air of a private palace. The rich fabrics and costumes displayed give a vivid idea of aristocratic living conditions in 17th- and 18th-century Venice.

Salizzada San Stae, Santa Croce. Tel: 04 172 1798. www.museiciviciveneziani.it. Open: Apr–Oct Tue–Sun 10am–5pm;

The lavish interior of Palazzo Mocenigo

Nov–Mar Tue–Sun 10am–4pm. Closed: Mon. Admission charge. Vaporetto: No 1 to San Stae.

Rialto

I will buy with you, sell with you, talk with you, walk with you, and so following; but I will not eat with you, drink with you, nor pray with you.
What news on the Rialto?
Shylock to Bassanio, *Merchant of Venice*, William Shakespeare.

From the islets of the lagoon, the first Venetian settlers gradually focused on an archipelago called the Rivus Altus. The islands, which had the advantage of a deep channel, became known as the Rialto. Strictly speaking, the term 'Rialto' is the quarter extending from the foot of the Rialto Bridge on the San Marco side of the Grand Canal to the Pescheria, or fish market.

The area has been a hub of commerce and trade since the end of the 11th century, when markets were first established here. During the heyday of the Republic, when Venice controlled all trade between East and West, traders from all corners of the civilised world assembled under the arcades of the Church of San Giacometto (*see pp69–70*) to trade in gold, spices, silks, fabrics and dyes. In 1514, the whole Rialto quarter, apart from the church, was devastated by fire. It was rebuilt shortly afterwards in a rather more functional style.

(*Cont. on p68*)

Walk: San Polo and Santa Croce

Beginning with a look at Venetian life in some of the humbler corners of the city, this walk goes on to explore the squares, streets and stalls of San Polo.

Allow 2 hours.

Start at the railway station. Cross the Scalzi Bridge, go straight ahead and then turn left over the Rio Marin. About 100m (328ft) along the quayside, turn left into Calle dei Croce, then right for Campo S Nazario Sauro. The street on the far side, Ruga Bella, will bring you into a large square.

1 Campo San Giacomo dell'Orio

Large, rambling, and dominated by its 9th-century church (*see p69*), the square is a focal point of Santa Croce. You can sit in the shade of plane trees and observe local life.

Head north along Calle Larga, cross the bridge and shortly turn right for Calle Tintor. The Salizzada San Stae leads to the church of the same name.

2 Church of San Stae

Overlooking the Grand Canal, San Stae has an exuberant Baroque façade, festooned with sculpture, and still looks pristine after its 1979 restoration (*Open: Mon–Sat 10am–5pm. Admission charge*).

Cross the little bridge and turn right then left, following signs for Ca' Pesaro (see pp60 & 62). Follow the Ca' Pesaro quayside and zigzag left and right to reach Campo Santa Maria Mater Domini.

3 Campo Santa Maria Mater Domini

This charming square has some fine medieval houses, a 14th-century well head and inviting outdoor cafés.

From the square, follow the Rialto signs as far as Campo San Cassiano.

4 Campo San Cassiano

More than 11,000 prostitutes were recorded in Venice in the 16th century, and the Campo San Cassiano was a notorious quarter for soliciting. Close by, the Ponte delle Tette (Bridge of the Breasts) is said to be named after the prostitutes who lured customers by stripping to the waist.

Take the narrow street on the far side of the church for Calle dei Boteri. Turn right along Calle dei Boteri. Before the

lesser paintings: *The Resurrection* and *Descent into Limbo*.
Campo San Cassiano, San Polo. Tel: 04 172 1408. Open: Tue–Sat 9am–noon. Vaporetto: No 1 to San Stae.

San Giacomo dell'Orio

The original 9th-century church was rebuilt in 1224. Despite constant alterations and renovations over the centuries, the interior is still medieval in atmosphere. This is largely due to the surviving basilica plan and the splendid Gothic ship's-keel roof. The very oldest features are a pair of columns looted from Byzantium.

The old sacristy is usually locked but you can peep through the bars to see the paintings by Palma il Giovane. The new sacristy contains ceiling paintings and an altarpiece by Veronese. Ask the custodian for entry.
Campo San Giacomo dell'Orio, Santa Croce. Tel: 041 275 0462. www. chorusvenezia.org. Open: Mon–Sat 10am–5pm. Admission charge. Vaporetto: No 1 to Riva di Biasio or San Stae.

San Giacomo di Rialto/ San Giacometto

This little church, surrounded by the hubbub of the market, is considered the oldest in Venice. Its foundations are said to go back to the time of the first settlement, in 421. The church you see

A complex cluster of buildings that makes up the Church of San Giacomo dell'Orio

today was built during the 11th and 12th centuries, then heavily restored in 1601. The large clock above the Gothic portico is renowned for its unreliability. Inside, the layout and proportions are still essentially Veneto-Byzantine.

Campo San Giacomo di Riatto, San Polo. Tel: 041 522 4745. Open: Mon–Sat 9.30am–noon & 4–5pm (no entry during Mass), Sun 11am–noon. Vaporetto: Nos 1 & 2 to Rialto or No 1 to Rialto Mercato.

San Giovanni Elemosinario

This 'invisible' church, hidden beneath the porticoes at Rialto – reopened after 25 years – boasts altarpieces painted by Titian and Pordenone which have been restored to their original glory at the Accademia galleries. The building was the work of Antonio Abbondì, alias Scarpagnino, and dates back to the aftermath of the disastrous 1514 fire that swept through the area.

Ruga Rialta, San Polo. Tel: 041 275 0462. www.chorusvenezia.org. Open: Mon–Sat 10am–5pm. Admission charge. Vaporetto: No 1 to San Silvestro or Rialto Mercato.

San Polo

Standing on the largest *campo* of the city, the Gothic Church of San Polo suffered heavy-handed restoration and restructuring in the early 19th century. The exterior's finest features are the Gothic portal and the detached 14th-century *campanile*, guarded at its base by two marble lions.

The interior houses Tintoretto's *Last Supper* (on the left as you go in) and Giandomenico Tiepolo's *Stations of the Cross*, in the Oratory of the Crucifix. Executed when Tiepolo was only 20 years of age, the series of paintings also includes portraits of Venetian society of the time. To study them all, you will need a good supply of coins for the lighting.

Campo San Polo, San Polo. Tel: 041 275 0462. www.chorusvenezia.org. Open: Mon–Sat 10am–5pm. Admission charge. Vaporetto: No 1 to San Silvestro.

San Rocco

On a small square by the Frari, the Church of San Rocco has a conspicuous façade, built in the 1760s and decorated with an abundance of statuary. Inside, the church boasts a number of works of art by Tintoretto. The most important of these are the four large canvases in the chancel, which depict scenes from the life of St Roch. Two of these show St Roch performing miracles, including *St Roch Healing the Plague Victims*.

Every 16 August, the doge would pay a visit to San Rocco Church, imploring the saint to protect the city from the plague. This event is re-enacted every year and visitors are allowed free entry to the Scuola (*see opposite*) on this day.

These Tintorettos, however, are minor works in comparison with the great cycle of paintings in the neighbouring Scuola Grande di San Rocco.

Campo San Rocco, San Polo. Tel: 041 523 4864. Open: daily 9.30am–

5.30pm. Vaporetto: Nos 1 & 2 to San Tomà.

Scuola Grande di San Rocco

Links with the East made Venice particularly susceptible to the bubonic plague. The Scuola San Rocco, founded in 1515 under the auspices of the patron saint of contagious diseases, became a charitable institution to nurse the sick and diseased. When an outbreak of the plague struck Venice in 1527, donations flowed into the Scuola from Venetians hoping to be saved from the epidemic by St Roch. The funds enabled the Scuola to finally complete its new building in 1560.

In 1564, a competition was held to decide which eminent artist should decorate the building. So eager was Tintoretto to win the commission that he persuaded his associates to smuggle in and install a full-sized panel of St Rocco, thereby infringing the judge's stipulation of a scaled model. Much to the wrath of his rivals, the work won him the competition.

Tintoretto took 23 years to complete the decoration of the Scuola. The result – some 50 large religious paintings – is not only a testimony to his distinctive art, but one of the supreme monuments to Italian Renaissance genius.

Detail from the façade of San Rocco Church

Exterior

The richly carved and decorated Renaissance façade (1516–49) was the work of both Bartolomeo Bon the younger (ground floor) and Antonio Scarpagnino (first floor).

Ground-floor hall

The paintings here consist of eight Tintoretto panels depicting scenes from the *Life of the Virgin Mary*. These last works, painted when the artist was nearing 70, show the mellowness of a mature man at one with the Christian message. To see them in life-cycle order, start at the top left-hand corner with *The Annunciation*, and go clockwise, ending with *The Assumption*. *St Mary Magdalene* and *St Mary of Egypt* are particularly noteworthy because here, unusually, Tintoretto allows the hazy, dream-like landscape to prevail over his figures.

Sala dell'Albergo (first floor)

To see the paintings in chronological order, start in the Sala dell'Albergo, reached by Scarpagnino's magnificent staircase. Off the upper hall, this room contains the first painting of the cycle, *The Crucifixion*. This huge work of art, demonstrating complex human emotions while conveying the single central drama of the Christian story, is the most moving and intensely dramatic of the collection.

On the ceiling is *St Roch in Glory*, the panel that won Tintoretto the commission. The three large paintings on the entrance wall, depicting the

Tintoretto's paintings in the Scuola have always attracted admiration. The great Florentine art historian Giorgio Vasari, when visiting the city two years after Tintoretto began his project, described him as 'the most extraordinary brain that the art of painting has produced'. Three centuries on, John Ruskin, the foremost art critic of his day in England, wrote after a visit to the Scuola, 'he took it so entirely out of me today that I could do nothing at last but lie on a bench and laugh'.

Passion of Christ, are dynamic and original, yet show the artist's expressive religious sensitivity. The easel painting of *Christ Carrying the Cross* once attributed to Giorgione, is now believed to be by Titian.

Upper hall

The paintings here were completed between 1576 and 1581. The ceiling consists of 13 panels of scenes from the Old Testament. The three square panels, *The Brazen Serpent*, *The Fall of Manna* and *Moses Striking Water from the Rock*, are allusions to man's relief from illness, hunger and thirst – all vital preoccupations of the Scuola. The huge wall paintings depict scenes from the life of Christ, where the theme is man's fight against spiritual evils. *The Nativity* and *The Temptation of Christ* are particularly notable for their movement and dramatic effect.

Campo San Rocco, San Polo. Tel: 041 523 4864. www.scuolagrandesanrocco.it. Open: daily 9.30am–5.30pm. Last entrance 30 minutes before closing. Admission charge. Vaporetto: Nos 1 & 2 to San Tomà.

The richly carved and decorated façade of the Scuola Grande di San Rocco

Dorsoduro

Dorsoduro – the 'solid back' of the city – sees the traditionally working-class west rubbing shoulders with the expat enclave to the east. Once one of the quieter parts of town, the district is now enjoying something of a renaissance, with new galleries, a thriving university area, and a generous serving of restaurants and bars. The district is a happy mix of raucous squares on a Saturday night and peaceful, sunny spots where you can soak up the daytime rays and ponder the city's delights.

Accademia

The Gallerie dell'Accademia (Accademia Galleries), housed in the former church, monastery and Scuola of the Santa Maria della Carità, are the repository of the world's most comprehensive collection of Venetian art. The works span five centuries and the masterpieces among them are far too numerous to absorb in one visit. Arrive as early as possible. The gallery was in the final stages of being extended and refurbished (to include a new café, for instance) at time of press. The rooms closed were IV, V, XIII, XVI, XVIA, XVII and XXIV, though many of the paintings from these rooms could be found in others. The highlights of the collection are:

Room I

The *Madonna with Child with Two Donors* and the polyptych of *The Coronation of the Virgin* by Paolo Veneziano show the heavy influence of the Byzantine. At the end of the room,

Michele Giambono's *Coronation of the Virgin* is a fine example of International Gothic, showing the leaning towards a more natural rendering of costume and details of nature.

Room II

Central to Venetian Renaissance art is the *Sacra Conversazione*, where the Madonna is portrayed in a unified composition with saints. An outstanding example of this theme is

VERONESE AND THE INQUISITION

In 1571 Titian's *Last Supper*, housed in the refectory of the Dominican monastery of Santi Giovanni e Paolo, was destroyed by fire. To replace it, Veronese was commissioned to paint another *Last Supper*. On its completion, the Inquisition objected to the profane content within a sacred subject. Veronese was ordered to eliminate the offending details, such as the animals and drunkards, the armed men dressed as Germans, and the jester with a parrot on his wrist. Rather than altering the painting, Veronese simply changed the title to the *Feast in the House of Levi*.

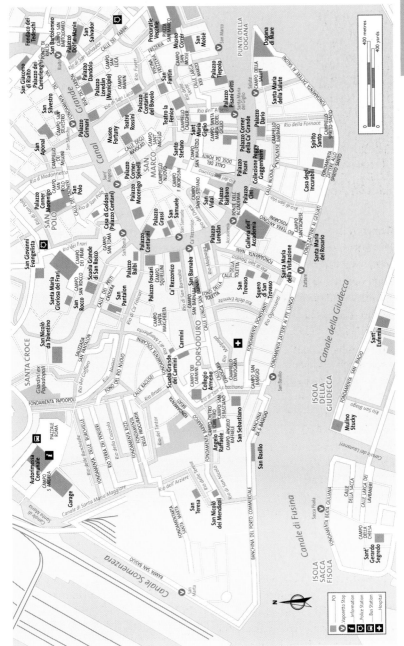

Dorsoduro

ISOLA
SACCA
FISOLA

Canale Scomenzera

RAMO SAN BASILIO

Canale di Santa Maria Maggiore

Canale di Fusina

SANTA CROCE

Giardini ex
Papadopoli

Fondamenta PAPADOPOLI

Garage

Autorimessa
Comunale

PIAZZALE
ROMA

CAMPO
S. ANDREA

FONDAMENTA DELLE BURCHIELLE

FONDAMENTA DELLE PENSIERI

Rio di Ca' Foscari

Rio Nuovo

FOND. DEL RIO NUOVO

SAN POLO

San Giovanni
Evangelista

Santa Maria
Gloriosa dei Frari

CAMPO
SAN ROCCO

CAMPO
DEI FRARI

Scuola Grande
di San Rocco

San
Rocco

CALLE DEI PRETI

CALLE LARGA FOSCARI

San
Pantalon

CAMPO
SAN TOMA

San
Nicolò
da Tolentino

San Nicolò
dei Mendicoli

San
Teresa

FONDAMENTA
SANTA MARTA

San
Sebastiano

Angelo il Tintoretto

CAMPO
ANGELO
RAFFAELE

San Basilio

BANCHINA
DI S. BIAGIO

Mulino
Stucky

ISOLA
DELLA
GIUDECCA

Canale della Giudecca

Sant'
Eufemia

FONDAMENTA SAN BIAGIO

Rio San Biago

Canale dei Lavraneri

CALLE LARGA DEI
LAVRANERI

CALLE
DELLA SACCA

FONDAMENTA BEATA GIULIANA

Sacca Fisola

CAMPO
DELLA
CHIESA

Sant'
Gerardo Segredo

San
Marta

BANCHINA DEL PORTO COMMERCIALE

DORSODURO

Scuola Grande
dei Carmini

Collegio
Armeno

Carmini

CAMPO
DEI CARMINI

CAMPO SAN
SEBASTIANO

CAMPIELLO
D'AVOGARIA

CAMPO SAN
BARNABA

Ca' Rezzonico

San Barnaba

CAMPO
SAN BARNABA

Palazzo
Balbi

Palazzo Foscari

Palazzo
Contarini

Casa di Goldoni
(Palazzo Centani)

Palazzo
Grassi

San
Samuele

Palazzo
Loredan

San
Vidal

Palazzo
Barbaro

Santo
Stefano

Palazzo
Pisani

CAMPO
SANTO STEFANO

Galleria dell'
Accademia

Santa Maria
della Visitazione

Squero di
San Trovaso

Santa Maria
del Rosario

Santa
Trovaso

PONTE
DELL'
ACCADEMIA

Accademia

FONDAMENTA ZATTERE AI GESUATI

Zattere

FONDAMENTA ZATTERE AI PONTE LUNGO

Canale della Giudecca

SAN
MARCO

Palazzo
Mocenigo

Palazzo
Corner-
Spinelli

Palazzo
Contarini

Campiello
F. Morosini

Santo
Stefano

Palazzo
Cini

Palazzo Corner
della Ca' Grande

Collezione Peggy
Guggenheim

Casa degli
Incurabili

CAMPO
SANTA
MARIA DEL
GIGLIO

Sant'
Maria
Giglio

Teatro la
Fenice

Teatro
Rossini

Palazzo
Grimani

Museo
Fortuny

San
Aponal

Palazzo
Corner

Palazzo
Moceigo

SAN POLO

CAMPO
SAN POLO

San
Polo

CAMPO SAN
SILVESTRO

San
Silvestro

San Giacomo
di Rialto

Palazzo dei
Camerlenghi

PONTE DI
RIALTO

Rialto

Canal Grande

Palazzo
Dandolo

Palazzo Dolfin-Manin

San
Salvador

Fondaco dei
Tedeschi

San Bartolomeo

Palazzo
Dolfin-Manin

CAMPO DI
SAN BARTOLOMEO

Palazzo
Loredan
(Municipio)

Palazzo
Contarini
del Bovolo

Palazzo
Manin

CAMPO
SAN LUCA

CAMPO
SAN FANTIN

Palazzo
Fantin

Procuratie
Vecchie

Museo
Correr

San
Moisè

Palazzo
Tiepolo

PIAZZA
SAN MARCO

Procuratie
Vecchie

CAMPO
SAN
MAURIZIO

Palazzo
Pisani Gritti

Santa Maria
del Giglio

Palazzo
Dario

Rio della Fornace

CAMPIELLO
BARBARO

Spirito
Santo

FONDAMENTA ZATTERE ALLO SPIRITO SANTO

PUNTA DELLA
DOGANA

Santa Maria
della Salute

Dogana
di Mare

CAMPO DELLA
SALUTE

FONDAMENTA ZATTERE AI SALONI

N

	POI
	Vaporetto Stop
	Information
	Police Station
	Bus Station
	Hospital

0 — 400 metres
0 — 400 yards

San Giobbe's altarpiece entitled *Madonna Enthroned with Saints* by the artist Giovanni Bellini.

Room IV

This and the following are two of the most important (and crowded) rooms in the gallery. Among the many masterpieces are *St George* by Mantegna, and the *Madonna and Child with St Catherine and Mary Magdalene* by Giovanni Bellini, the greatest of the Venetian Madonna painters.

Room V

Giorgione's mysterious *Tempest*, poetic yet humanistic in its vision, is one of the most famous paintings in the canon

One of the world's greatest art galleries

of Western art. The subject, however, still remains a mystery. Masterpieces by Giovanni Bellini include the *Madonna of the Little Trees*, the *Pietà*, and the sublime *Madonna and Child between St John the Baptist and a Female Saint*, which demonstrate the artist's ability to bring together figures and landscape in perfect harmony.

Rooms VI, VII and VIII

These three rooms concentrate on the early 16th century when the Venetian Renaissance was well into its stride. Lorenzo Lotto's slightly melancholic *Gentleman in his Study* typifies Venetian psychological penetration in portraiture, while Titian's *St John the Baptist* exemplifies Venetian artists' sensual humanistic approach to religious subjects. Close to ceiling level is Paolo Veronese's *Venice Receives Homage from Hercules and Ceres*, exemplary in its use of colour and light effects.

Room X

Occupying an entire wall is Paolo Veronese's *Feast in the House of Levi*, renamed after the painter faced the Inquisition, accused of profanity. Tintoretto's tumultuous *St Mark Freeing a Slave* was the first of the canvases he executed for the Scuola Grande di San Marco. His extraordinary ability to convey theatrical effect through contrasts of light and shade and bold foreshortening is also demonstrated in *The Stealing of the Body of St Mark* and *St Mark Saving a Saracen*. Titian's dark *Pietà* was the last of his works, finished by Palma il Giovane.

Room XI

The room contains further works by Tintoretto, notably, a crowned *Crucifixion*, dating back to the period when he was influenced by Paolo Veronese's work. Although Baroque painting never excelled in Venice, the 18th century saw the emergence of the prolific talent of Giovanni Battista Tiepolo (1696–1770), the leading European decorative painter of his time. Examples of his brilliant illusionistic perspective and his chromatic luministic effects can be seen in his frescoes and frieze detached from suppressed churches, and other works in Rooms XV–XVII.

Rooms XII–XVII

Room XII is packed with 18th-century works of serene romanticism and dramatic fantasy. Rooms XV–XVII contain works by Longhi, Tiepolo, Canaletto and Guardi.

Accademia: ceremonial paintings

Rooms XX and XXI contain two cycles of paintings, called *teleri*, which capture some of the vital elements of Venice at the end of the 15th century. The greatest ceremonial painters of the day were Gentile Bellini, brother of Giovanni, and Vittore Carpaccio. Their grand-scale, minutely detailed works of art give a fascinating insight into Venetian life and customs of the time. They also demonstrate the Venetian love of pageantry and their preoccupation with the sacred and the saints, brought to life in a way which was graphic and human.

Room XX: The stories of the Cross

In 1369, the Kingdom of Cyprus donated to the Scuola of San Giovanni Evangelista a relic of the Holy Cross. The cycle of eight *teleri*, each one commemorating an incident concerning the sacred relic, was commissioned by the Scuola. Gentile Bellini's *Procession in St Mark's Square* (1496) depicts an episode when the dying son of a Brescian merchant recovers as his father kneels before the relic. His *Miracle of the Cross at Ponte San Lorenzo* (1500) recalls an event when the relic fell into the canal and escaped the grasp of everybody except the Scuola's senior guardian.

Carpaccio's *Miracle of the True Cross at the Rialto Bridge* (1494) shows the old wooden bridge which collapsed in 1524. On the left, on the upper balcony, is a madman, reputedly healed during this miracle with the relic.

Room XXI: The story of St Ursula

Painted for the Scuola di Sant'Ursola in the 1490s, these canvases make up one of the most graphic pieces of secular narrative painting to emerge from 15th-century Italy. The scenes tell the

(*Cont. on p80*)

Renaissance art in Venice

Renaissance painting came late to Venice. On account of the Republic's strong links with the Orient and its dogged individualism, Byzantine and Gothic styles lingered well into the 15th century. But when the Renaissance did come to Venice, it flourished. Light and colour were its touchstones, in contrast to line and form in rival Florence. The approach was primarily unintellectual, the vibrant spirit of Venice imbuing Renaissance art with its own sparkling qualities.

Giovanni Bellini (c.1430–1516) was the leader in bringing Venetian

Portrait of Titian, engraved after a drawing by William Fairland

Renaissance painting to its pinnacle. He grew up at a time when some of the great Florentine artists, such as Paolo Uccello, Fra Filippo Lippi and Donatello, were working in Padua and Venice. His brother-in-law, Andrea Mantegna (1431–1506), who worked in Padua and then Mantua, was highly influential in his controlled, rational style and mastery of perspective and foreshortening. Giovanni Bellini added humanity to Mantegna's harsh realism, and his Madonnas are unsurpassed in their warmth, harmony and sheer beauty.

Bellini in turn influenced other great masters. One was the enigmatic Giorgione (1477/8–1510), who died of the plague in his early 30s but whose creative imagination and innovative approach to light and colour made him a forerunner of modern painting.

Titian (1485–1576), who achieved an unrivalled mastery of rich colour and harmonious composition, became the most sought-after painter in Europe. During his long life (he was still painting vigorously in his 80s), he enjoyed patronage from doges and royalty.

Two great masters who vied with Titian were Paolo Veronese (1528–88), who achieved stunning effects by his use of luminosity and colour, and the passionate and prolific Jacopo Tintoretto (1518–94), who

Detail from a portrait of Giovanni Bellini (anon), 1850

developed a dazzling personal style through his profound mastery of dramatic light effects.

The city of Venice is renowned not only for the sensuality it gave to Renaissance painting, but also for the fact that here the Renaissance endured. Long after the sack of Rome (1527) and the dead hand of the Counter-Reformation had ended the Renaissance as a coherent Italian phenomenon, vigorous independent Venice continued the great event.

story of Ursula, daughter of the Christian king of Brittany, who agreed to marry the pagan son of the king of England on condition that he would convert to Christianity and she could make a pilgrimage to Rome with 11,000 virgins. The consequence was the martyrdom of Ursula and her maidens at the hands of the Huns.

Room XXIII bis

These cavernous former church premises house the glorious series painted for the Sala dell'Albergo of the Scuola Grande di San Marco, with Paris Bordon's brilliant *The Fisherman and the Doge*, not to mention works by Giovanni Bellini. Temporary exhibitions are held here as well.

Room XXIV

Titian's *Presentation of the Virgin*, occupying the exact spot for which it was painted, makes a fitting finale to the galleries.

The Accademia is located in Campo della Carità, Dorsoduro. Tel: 041 520 0345 (call centre). www.gallerieaccademia.org. Open: Mon 8.15am–2pm, Tue–Sun 8.15am–7.15pm. Ticket office closes at 6.45pm. Admission charge. Vaporetto: Nos 1 & 2 to Accademia.

Ca' Rezzonico

A monumental Baroque palace on the Grand Canal, the recently restored Ca' Rezzonico was designed for the patrician Filippo Bon by the leading

The loggia of Ca' Rezzonico

Venetian architect Baldassare Longhena. Work began in 1667, but funds ran out, and it was not until 1756 (long after both Longhena and Bon were dead) that the palace was completed.

By this time, the palace had passed into the hands of the Rezzonicos, an enormously rich, non-aristocratic family from the mainland who had bought their way into Venetian nobility. In the decoration of the palace, and the feasts that were subsequently held there, no expense was spared.

In the late 19th century, Robert Browning's reprobate son, Pen, redeemed himself by purchasing the palace (albeit through the funds of his wealthy American heiress wife) and refurbishing it on a regal scale. Robert Browning, who was to have 'a corner for his old age', died of bronchitis just a few weeks after its completion. The funeral service was held in the hall of the palace.

Since 1936, Ca' Rezzonico has housed the **Museo del Settecento Veneziano** (Museum of 18th-century Venice). Many of the furnishings, paintings and even entire ceilings have been taken from other *palazzi*, but the overall effect is homogeneous, the size and grandeur of the rooms giving a fascinating insight into a life of luxury on the Grand Canal in the 18th century.

Exterior

The façade is decorated with columns, balustrades and a proliferation of sculptural detail. Henry James described the palace as 'thrusting itself upon the water with a peculiar florid assurance, a certain upward toss of its cornice which gives it the air of a rearing sea horse'.

Piano nobile

A formidable stone stairway leads up to the *piano nobile*. A fitting introduction to the interior is the magnificent ballroom, decorated with *trompe-l'œil* frescoes, vast chandeliers and elaborate ebonised furniture crafted by Andrea Brustolon. In the room on the right of the ballroom is a ceiling frescoed by Giovanni Battista Tiepolo, depicting the allegorical marriage in 1758 of a

Rezzonico into the fabulously wealthy and influential Savorgnan family.

Second floor

The second floor is primarily devoted to 18th-century paintings. The collection includes one of the very few surviving paintings by Canaletto in Venice.

Do not miss the Sala dei Longhi, showing more than 30 charming scenes of late 18th-century Venetian life. These include portraits of patrician families, doughnut sellers, alchemists, washerwomen and the notorious rhinoceros that came to the city in 1779.

A room overlooking the Grand Canal displays two Guardi paintings, one depicting masked gamblers in the Ridotto, the other showing nuns in their parlour at the San Zaccaria convent.

The last rooms are decorated with delightful, light-hearted frescoes by

(*Cont. on p84*)

CANALETTO (1697–1768)

It was in the 1720s that Antonio Canal, better known as Canaletto, began painting the Venetian scenes that were to make him one of the most famous 18th-century *Vedutisti*, or topographical painters. The earlier scenes, many painted on the spot, are characterised by free handling and strong contrasts of light and shade. Later, he returned to the traditional method of painting from drawings, and his works became harder, tighter and generally less alluring.

He worked largely for the English market in Venice, and therefore, sadly, there are very few of his works to be seen in Venice today.

Walk: Dorsoduro

This is a scenic stroll through southern Venice, combining picturesque streets and squares with fine panoramas.

Allow 2 hours or more, excluding sightseeing.

Start at the foot of the Accademia Bridge facing the buildings housing the Accademia Galleries (see pp74, 76–7 & 80). Walk eastwards, following signs for the Peggy Guggenheim Collection (see pp84–5), and continue through the delightful Campiello Barbaro, towards the Salute Church (see pp86 & 88). Follow the fondamenta to the eastern tip of the Dorsoduro.

1 Punta della Dogana

After years of standing empty and forlorn, the Punta della Dogana came under intense bidding between two big-hitters in the art world: the Guggenheim Collection and Henri Francois Pinault. The latter won and has transformed the old customs house into a showcase for contemporary art, much of which comes from his own private collection. From here, savour the stunning 180-degree panorama, taking in San Marco, San Giorgio Maggiore and Giudecca.
Campo della Salute, Dorsoduro. Tel: 199 139 139 (from Italy) or
0039 044 523 0313 (ticket office). www.palazzograssi.it. Open: Wed–Mon 10am–7pm. Admission charge. Joint tickets for the Punta and Palazzo Grassi available.
Walk round the headland to reach the southern quay of the Dorsoduro.

2 Zattere

Boats once offloaded their goods on the *zattere* (wooden rafts) that lined the quayside. Flagstones replaced the rafts in the early 16th century. Today, it has the air of a sunny promenade, with fine views across to the island of Giudecca.
Pass the Gesuati Church (see p86), then turn right at the Rio di San Trovaso, keeping to this side of the canal.

3 Squero di San Trovaso

Across the water, the wooden chalet-like building is one of the city's last surviving gondola boatyards. New boats are made here (about ten a year, costing around €25,000 a piece) and old ones are regularly fixed up.

Cross the second bridge and follow the flow to Campo San Barnaba.

4 Campo San Barnaba

The barge by the bridge is one of the few floating vegetable barges remaining in Venice. On the bridge itself, two pairs of footprints mark the spot where brawls took place between the rival city groups of the Castellani and Nicolotti – hence the name, Ponte dei Pugni (Bridge of Fists).

Walk westwards along Calle Lunga San Barnaba, passing small shops and artisans. Cross the bridge at the end for San Sebastiano Church (see pp88–9). Continue west via the campo *and Church of San Angelo Raffaele. Cross the Rio di San Nicolò and continue along this canal.*

5 San Nicolò dei Mendicoli

According to popular tradition, the church was founded in the 7th century and given the name of Mendicoli (beggars) because of the poverty of the area. What you see today is a small, intimate church dating from the 12th century, which was lovingly restored by the Venice in Peril Fund in the mid-1970s. The main works of art are the wooden sculptures and paintings in the nave, by pupils of Veronese, of *The Life of Christ.* The church is open daily, 10am–noon and 4–6pm.

Retrace your steps back to San Sebastiano, cross the bridge, and follow the canal southwards to the Zattere. Vaporetto Nos 2 & 61/62 from San Basilio will take you in either direction.

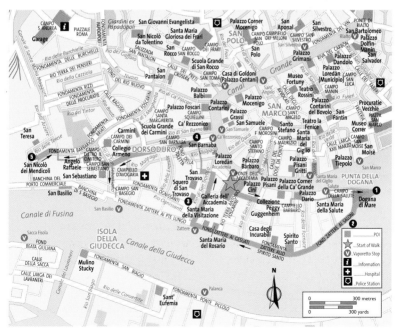

Giandomenico Tiepolo (son of Giovanni Battista), featuring carnival scenes and clowns. *Il Mondonuovo* (The New World) depicts Venetian crowds watching a peepshow at a Sunday fair, and among the onlookers are the artist and his father.

Third floor

The most interesting exhibit on this floor is the reconstruction of an 18th-century apothecary shop from Campo San Stin.

Museo del Settecento Veneziano: Fondamenta Rezzonico, Dorsoduro 3136. Tel: 041 241 0100. www.museiciviciveneziani.it. Open: Apr–Oct Wed–Mon 10am–6pm; Nov–Mar Wed–Mon 10am–5pm. Admission charge (ticket office closes an hour earlier). Vaporetto: No 1 to Ca' Rezzonico.

Campo dei Carmini
Carmini (Santa Maria del Carmelo)

This is a grandiose, if forbidding, church and its most prominent features are the black-and-gold figures of kings, saints, warriors and bishops along the arches of the nave. Above them, a painted frieze depicts stories from the history of the Carmelite order. The dark-looking *Nativity* by Cima da Conegliano on the second altar on the right can be brought to life with a coin. The other major work of art, on the other side of the nave, is the altarpiece of *St Nicholas of Bari with Saints Lucy and John the Baptist* by Lorenzo Lotto.

Campo dei Carmini, Dorsoduro. Tel: 041 270 2464. www.scuolagrandecarmini.it. Open: Mon–Sat 2.30–5pm. Vaporetto: No 1 to Ca' Rezzonico.

Scuola Grande dei Carmini

Built in 1668 to a design by Longhena, the Scuola was the headquarters of the prestigious Brotherhood of the Carmelites. It is full of 18th-century paintings, but what most people come to see is Tiepolo's ceiling in the upper hall. Painted in the 1740s, it comprises nine canvases focusing on the central scene of *St Simon Stock Receiving the Scapular of the Carmelite Order from the Virgin*.
Campo Carmini, Dorsoduro. Tel: 041 528 9420. www.scuolagrandecarmini.it. Open: daily 11am–4pm. Admission charge. Vaporetto: No 1 to Ca' Rezzonico.

Campo Santa Margherita

Campo Santa Margherita is a focal point of the Dorsoduro. Housewives come for the fish, fruit and vegetable stalls, university students for the bars, pizzerias and second-hand book stalls, while tourists are normally making for the church and Scuola of the Carmini (*see above*), southwest of the square. Café Causin, at No 2996, serves particularly good home-made ice creams.

Collezione Peggy Guggenheim

Palazzo Venier dei Leoni was originally conceived as a grand four-storey palace,

Marino Marini's *Angelo della Città* stands provocatively on the Guggenheim terrace

Solomon R Guggenheim New York Foundation, which turned the palace into a museum of modern art.

Light, airy rooms overlooking the Grand Canal make an appropriate setting for the 20th-century canvases. Leading artists represented here include Picasso, de Chirico, Rothko, Magritte, Chagall, Mondrian, Kandinsky and Malevich.

A whole room is devoted to Jackson Pollock, one of Peggy Guggenheim's many discoveries. Among the artists were Guggenheim's friends, lovers and – in the case of Max Ernst – husband.

The garden, which borders the Grand Canal, is studded with sculpture, the most eye-catching piece being the blatantly erotic *Angelo della Città* by Marino Marini. Peggy Guggenheim's grave (along with the graves of her nine dogs) takes backstage in the garden of the palace.

The museum has recently been extended to include a café/restaurant and a shop.

Palazzo Venier dei Leoni, Fondamenta Venier dei Leoni 708, Dorsoduro.
Tel: 041 240 5411.
www.guggenheim-venice.it.
Open: Wed–Mon 10am–6pm.
Admission charge. Vaporetto: Nos 1 & 2 to Accademia.

intended to outdo the huge Palazzo Corner della Ca' Grande, which it faces across the Grand Canal – but it never rose beyond the first storey. Designed by the neoclassical architect Lorenzo Boschetti, the squat, white building, which could not look less like a Venetian Grand Canal palace, acquired the name of Il Palazzo Nonfinito (The Unfinished Palace).

Peggy Guggenheim, one of the great contemporary art collectors of the 20th century, bought Palazzo Venier dei Leoni in 1949: she transferred her entire collection of art to the palace, and lived here until she died in 1979. The collection is managed by the

Galleria di Palazzo Cini (Palazzo Cini Gallery)

The exhibits form part of the private collection of Count Vittorio Cini (1884–1977), who established the Cini

Foundation on the island of San Giorgio Maggiore. Paintings, manuscripts, porcelain, furniture and ivories are displayed in the rooms of his former home by the Rio di San Vio. The collection is particularly strong on Tuscan art, and includes paintings by Botticelli, Piero della Francesca, Filippo Lippi, Bernardo Daddi, Piero di Cosimo and Pontormo.

In the neighbouring Campo San Vio, the wooden bench by the waterside makes an excellent vantage point over the Grand Canal.

San Vio, Dorsoduro. Tel: 041 521 0755. www.cini.it/palazzocini/home.html. Opening times vary. Admission charge. Vaporetto: Nos 1 & 2 to Accademia.

Gesuati (Santa Maria del Rosario)

The Gesuati church was built for the Dominicans in the first half of the 18th century. The most striking work of art is the frescoed ceiling showing scenes from the life of St Dominic, by Tiepolo. This is an early work, but one that already demonstrates the artist's mastery of light and perspective. The altar paintings worth picking out are Tiepolo's *Virgin and Child with Saints* (first altar on the right), G B Piazzetta's *Tre Santi* (third altar on the right) and Tintoretto's dramatically lit *Crucifixion* (third altar on the left).

The neighbouring **Santa Maria della Visitazione**, a very elegant little Renaissance church built by the Gesuati, has been fully restored in recent years.

Zattere, Dorsoduro. Tel: 041 275 0462.

www.chorusvenezia.org. Open: Mon–Sat 10am–5pm, Sun 1–5pm. Admission charge. Vaporetto: Nos 41/42, 51/52, 61/62 & 2 to Zattere.

Salute (Santa Maria della Salute)

The plague which struck Venice and the lagoon in 1630 took around 95,000 lives. A vow was made that a church would be dedicated to the Virgin Mary if she delivered the city from the epidemic. The plague ended in 1631, and Baldassare Longhena, then only 33 years of age, was chosen to design the Church of Salute (meaning 'health'). It took over half a century to build and was not consecrated until after his death. According to 17th-century records, 1,106,657 piles of oak, alder and larch were used for the foundations.

Exterior

A huge domed Baroque church, the Salute is dramatically located at the entrance of the Grand Canal. Along with San Marco and San Giorgio Maggiore, it is the most painted church in Venice, captured on canvas by Canaletto, Guardi and numerous other great and not-so-great painters. To Henry James, the church was 'like some great lady on the threshold of her salon…with her domes and scrolls, her scalloped buttresses and statues forming a pompous crown, and her wide steps disposed on the ground like the train of a robe.' To appreciate this architectural extravaganza you should ideally view the façade from the Grand

Santa Maria della Salute cuts an impressive profile

Canal. Campo della Salute and the steps of the church are far too close to take in the whole façade with all its ornamentation.

Interior

First seen from the side entrance, the grey and white interior lacks the theatricality of the façade; but seen from the main door, as Longhena intended, it creates a far greater impact. (The only time this door is open is for the Festa della Salute; *see p17*.) The great dome of the church, which symbolises the crown of the Virgin, is supported by eight pillars and surrounded by side chapels. Giusto Le Court's finely carved sculpture at the high altar shows the Virgin saving Venice from an ugly old woman who represents the plague. The most notable paintings are concentrated in the sacristy, to the left of the main altar: Titian's altarpiece, *St Mark Enthroned with Saints Cosmos, Damian, Roch and Sebastian*, and on the ceiling, in dramatic perspective, his fully restored Old Testament scenes of *Cain and Abel, Abraham and Isaac* and *David and Goliath*. Tintoretto's festive *Marriage at Cana*, to the right of the altar, was praised by Ruskin as a picture which 'unites colour as rich as Titian's with light and shade as forcible as Rembrandt's, and far more decisive'. *Campo della Salute, Dorsoduro. Tel: 041 274 3911. Open: daily 9am– noon & 3–5.30pm. Admission charge to sacristy only. Vaporetto: No 1 to Salute.*

San Pantalon

The most striking features of this late 17th-century church are the unfinished brick façade, and the spectacular ceiling paintings which represent the life and martyrdom of the physician St Pantalon, and are remarkable for their illusionistic perspective. It took Gian Antonio Fumiani 24 years to complete these 40 panels – and then he fell to his death from the scaffolding.

The second chapel on the right houses one of Veronese's last works, *San Pantalon Healing a Boy*. Within the Chapel of the Holy Nail, to the left of the chancel, is the painting *Coronation of the Virgin* (1444), by Antonio Vivarini and Giovanni d'Alemagna. *Campo San Pantalon, Dorsoduro. Tel: 041 270 2464. Open: Mon–Sat 10am–noon & 1–3pm, Thur 9–10.30pm. Vaporetto: Nos 1 & 2 to San Tomà.*

San Sebastiano

Thanks to Veronese, this is one of the most delightful small churches in Venice. It was built between 1505 and 1545 and designed by Scarpagnino. The interior is an art gallery of Veronese's paintings – glowing, joyous works which decorate ceiling, frieze, choir, altarpiece, organ doors and sacristy. The most famous of these works are the ceiling paintings depicting *The Story of Esther*.

Fittingly, Veronese is buried in the church; his tombstone lies near the organ.

Rio di San Sebastiano, Dorsoduro. Tel: 041 275 0462. www.chorus venezia.org. Open: Mon–Sat 10am–5pm. Admission charge. Vaporetto: Nos 2 & 61/62 to San Basilio.

San Trovaso

Distinctive for its twin Palladian façades, the Church of San Trovaso occupies a peaceful spot beside a canal, in the Dorsoduro. The highlights inside are the delightful Gothic painting of *Saint Chrysogonus on Horseback* by Michele Giambono in the chapel on the right of the high altar, and in the chapel opposite, the 15th-century marble relief of angels, decorating the altar-front. *Campo San Trovaso, Dorsoduro. Tel: 041 522 2133. Open: Mon–Sat 8–11am & 2.30–5.30pm, Sun 8–9.30am. Vaporetto: Nos 2, 51/52 & 61/62 to Zattere, or Nos 1 & 2 to Accademia.*

Santi Gervasio e Protasio – shortened to San Trovaso in Venetian dialect

Tour: Grand Canal

The No 1 waterbus is the slow boat down the Grand Canal, stopping at every landing stage. This enables you to sit back and admire the parade of palazzi *that line the banks. The trip takes you from San Marco to Piazzale Roma and back again, giving time to focus on palaces on both banks. See the Grand Canal map on p93 for the boat's route, and for more information on the Grand Canal, see pp35 & 38.*

Allow about an hour.

Take a No 1 vaporetto *from San Zaccaria or San Marco; try to sit on the left-hand side of the boat.*

LEFT BANK
1 Salute
This is the finest Baroque church of the city – a monumental building with a huge central dome and an exuberance of scrolls and statues (*see pp86 & 88*).

2 Palazzo Dario
Almost opposite the Santa Maria del Giglio landing stage (right bank) stands the leaning Palazzo Dario, distinctive for its inlaid marble façade and old-fashioned chimneypots. Past owners include the French poet Henri de Regnier, who lived here at the end of the last century, and Woody Allen got married here.

3 Palazzo Venier dei Leoni
The incongruous Palazzo Venier dei Leoni is also known as Palazzo Nonfinito because it never got beyond

one storey. The palace houses the Peggy Guggenheim Collection.

4 Ponte dell'Accademia
Replacing a heavy iron structure, the wooden Accademia Bridge was built in the 1930s as a temporary structure. However, the Venetians grew so fond of it that the bridge was retained. It is named after the Accademia Galleries, housed in the former monastery and Scuola of the Santa Maria della Carità.

5 Ca' Rezzonico
Just beyond the next stop, the vast Ca' Rezzonico was designed by Longhena in the 17th century, but not completed until many years after the architect's death. It now houses the Museum of 18th-century Venice (*see p81*).

6 Ca' Foscari
Described by John Ruskin as 'the noblest example in Venice of 15th-century Gothic', this was built in 1437

for Doge Francesco Foscari. It is now part of the university premises.

7 Palazzo Balbi

On the curve of the canal and distinctive for its pinnacles, the large late Renaissance Palazzo Balbi occupies a prime position. It was from here that Napoleon watched the regatta of 1807, held in his honour.

8 Ponte di Rialto

After the collapse of two wooden drawbridges across the Grand Canal, plans were drawn up for a stronger stone structure to span the canal. Michelangelo, Palladio and Sansovino were among the eminent contenders for the commission, but in the end it was the suitably named Antonio da Ponte who won. The present bridge was built from 1588 to 1591.

9 Palazzo dei Camerlenghi

Situated immediately after the Rialto, this handsome palace was once the home of the *camerlenghi* (city treasurers); then in the 16th century, it served as the state prison. Beyond the palace, morning market stalls are laid out under the arcaded Fabbriche Vecchie.

10 Ca' Pesaro

Beyond the Ca' d'Oro stop, the large building jutting into the canal on the left bank is the Ca' Pesaro, another Baroque palace by Longhena. Housed here are the Galleria Internationale d'Arte Moderna and the Museo d'Arte Orientale (*see pp60 & 62*).

11 Fondaco dei Turchi

This building in Veneto-Byzantine style was leased to Turkish merchants as a warehouse and living quarters. Almost entirely reconstructed in the 19th century, it now houses the Natural History Museum (*see pp64–5*).
The vaporetto *passes under the Ponte degli Scalzi and stops at both the railway station and Piazzale Roma. There is nothing stopping you from staying aboard for the return journey to San Marco, if you have purchased a 'Grand Canal' ticket that lasts 90 minutes.*

Ca' Rezzonico now houses the Museum of 18th-century Venice

RIGHT BANK
12 Church of the Scalzi

Located just beyond the railway station, this Baroque church is named after the Scalzi, the 'barefoot' Carmelite friars who founded it in the 17th century. In 1915, an Austrian bomb shattered the roof and Tiepolo's ceiling fresco. However, fragments of the ceiling are now in the Accademia Galleries.

13 Palazzo Vendramin Calergi

Beyond Rio di San Marcuola is this splendid and very prominent Renaissance palace. Mauro Coducci designed it in the 15th century and the Lombardo workshop completed it in 1509. Wagner died here in 1883. It now houses the casino (*www.casinovenezia.it*).

14 Ca' d'Oro (House of Gold)

Two stops further on is the famous Ca' d'Oro. Originally it was covered in gold leaf. Today, it houses the Franchetti collection of art (*see pp94 & 96–7*).

15 Fondaco dei Tedeschi

Immediately before the Rialto Bridge, the porticoed Fondaco dei Tedeschi was a warehouse used by the Germans of the 1300s. The façade must have looked far more splendid in the days when it was decorated with frescoes by Giorgione and Titian.

16 Palazzo Dandolo

Beyond the Rialto landing stages – and squeezed between more substantial *palazzi* – this marks the birthplace of Doge Enrico Dandolo. In 1204, 90 years old and blind, he masterminded the sack of Constantinople.

17 Palazzo Grimani

After the San Silvestro stop, you will see the austere-looking Palazzo Grimani, a Renaissance masterpiece by Michele Sanmicheli, now housing the Court of Appeal.

18 Palazzo Corner-Spinelli

Just before the Sant'Angelo stop, the Corner-Spinelli is arguably the finest Renaissance palace in Venice. The building is distinctive for its round-headed, double-arched windows and rusticated ground floor.

19 Palazzo Mocenigo

Opposite the San Tomà landing stage, the residences making up Palazzo Mocenigo were built for the wealthy Mocenigo family. Byron rented the palace for £200 a year, wrote poetry here and was pampered by a dozen servants. Byron's affair with the housekeeper ended dramatically with the brandishing of knives – and then his lover cast herself into the Grand Canal.

20 Palazzo Grassi

Just before the San Samuele stop, this is an 18th-century palace which was bought and restored by the Fiat car company as a venue for major art exhibitions. Now owned by French billionaire François Pinault, it opened as a major modern art gallery in 2006 (*see p49*).

21 Palazzo Barbaro

The second and third buildings beyond the Accademia Bridge are the Gothic Barbaro palaces. The far one was renowned for the illustrious guests who stayed here when it belonged to the Curtis family of Boston, including Robert Browning, Claude Monet, John Singer Sargent, James Whistler and Henry James, who wrote *The Aspern Papers* while he was here.

22 Palazzo Corner della Ca' Grande

Opposite the one-storey Palazzo Venier dei Leoni, this handsome classical

palace was built by Sansovino for the immensely rich Corner family.

23 Palazzo Pisani-Gritti

The 15th-century palace belonged to Doge Andrea Gritti, linguist, politician, militarist and womaniser. Somerset Maugham wrote from the terrace: 'Few things in the world are as charming as sitting here while the sun goes down and bathes the Salute in vivid colour.'

24 Ca' Contarini-Fasan

Opposite the Salute stop, this tiny but exquisite 15th-century house is known as the House of Desdemona, although Shakespeare's character was murdered before the building was even built, adding mystery to its ownership.

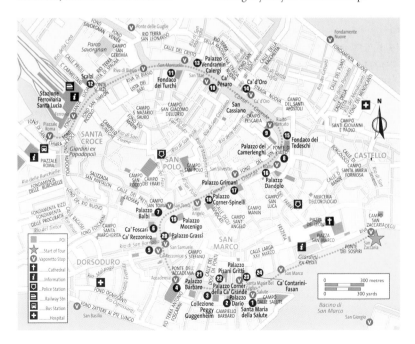

Cannaregio

Despite the waves of tourists flowing into Venice, many of them arriving directly in this district via the train station, Cannaregio has managed to retain a low-key profile. All you have to do to enjoy this neighbourhood is to steer clear of Rio Terrà Lista di Spagna and Strada Nuova (unless you're here for the shops) and seek out the quieter stretches of canalsides and calli *(streets) leading to breathtaking churches and sumptuous palaces.*

Ca' d'Oro

Overlooking the Grand Canal, the ornate façade of this palace was once so heavily adorned with gold leaf, vermilion and ultramarine that the building was named Ca' d'Oro (House of Gold). The intricate, lace-like façade has been preserved and is regarded as the most beautiful Gothic palace exterior in Venice. The modernised interior houses the Giorgio Franchetti Gallery of paintings, sculpture and furniture.

Renovations, old and new

The sumptuous palace was built for a wealthy Venetian patrician between 1425 and 1440. The work was carried out by Lombard craftsmen under the Milanese stonemason Matteo Raverti and, later, by Venetians under Giovanni Bon and his son. The site had previously been occupied by a Byzantine palace, and parts of this were preserved within the ornate façade of the Ca' d'Oro.

The palace has suffered heavy-handed changes over the centuries. The worst offender was 19th-century ballet dancer Maria Taglioni, who was given the palace as a gift by the Russian Prince Alexander Troubetskoy, and ripped out the staircases, street portal and much of the stonework.

The illustrious Baron Franchetti restored the palace in 1894 and gave it to the state, along with his paintings, sculpture, tapestries and other antiquities. While living at the palace, Franchetti planned a gallery, but he was suffering from an incurable disease, and took his own life in 1922. The palace, opened as an art gallery in 1927.

Recently, the Ca' d'Oro was closed for 15 years for a massive, and somewhat controversial, project of restoration and modernisation. Inside, it now feels more like a modern art gallery than a 15th-century palace. The exterior, masked behind scaffolding for five years, now reveals some of the colour which originally adorned the façade.

For Walk route see pp100–101

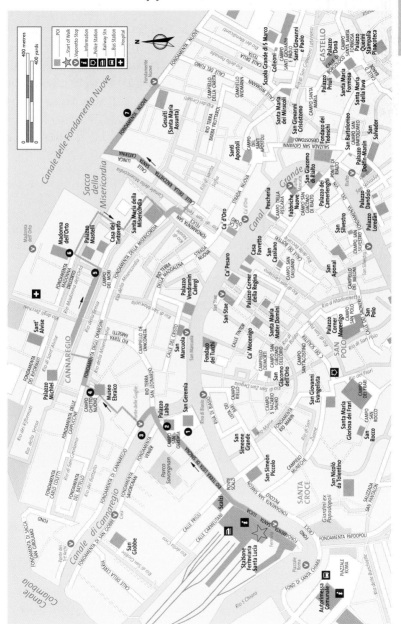

Courtyard

The main courtyard has a finely carved well head in red Verona marble by Bartolomeo Bon. Resembling a large capital, it is decorated with acanthus leaves and carved allegorical figures of Fortitude, Justice and Charity. The well head was sold by Maria Taglioni but recovered, along with the staircase in the courtyard and other pieces of the palace, by Baron Franchetti.

First floor

Franchetti's most prized painting, Mantegna's very expressive *St Sebastian*, is displayed in its own little 'chapel' on the first floor. This was Mantegna's last executed work before he died in 1506.

Opening on to the Grand Canal, the Portego, or main gallery, is lined with some notable classical and Renaissance Venetian bas-reliefs and sculpture, including the finely executed double portrait of *The Young Couple* by Tullio Lombardo and the delightful *Madonna and Child* marble lunette by Sansovino.

The rooms off the galleries have medallions by Pisanello, a collection of paintings by early Venetian and non-Venetian artists, and further displays of Renaissance sculpture. At the end of the gallery, you can look out through the arches on to the Grand Canal.

Second floor

Reached by way of an intricately carved 15th-century wooden staircase, the upper floor contains some minor works by leading Venetians, including

The Ca' d'Oro – universally admired as the finest Gothic façade in the city

fragments of frescoes by Titian which once adorned the outer walls of the Fondaco dei Tedeschi. These were removed for reasons of preservation.

Other works on this floor include Van Dyck's *Portrait of a Gentleman*, two views of Venice attributed to Guardi, and fresco fragments by Pordenone, which were recovered from the cloisters of the Church of Santo Stefano.

There are also huge Flemish tapestries and masses of ceramics, along with more glorious views of the Grand Canal.

Galleria Franchetti: Canal Grande, Cannaregio (off Strada Nova).

Tel: 041 520 0345 (call centre). www. cadoro.org. Open: Mon 8.15am–2pm, Tue–Sun 8.15am–7.15pm. Ticket office closes half an hour before the official closing time. Admission charge. Facilities include a bookshop selling postcards and posters of exhibitions. Vaporetto: No 1 to Ca' d'Oro.

Gesuiti (Santa Maria Assunta)

The Jesuits' devotion to the Counter-Reformation did not endear them to the Venetians, and it was only in 1715 that they were allowed to build their own church in Venice. In their determination to make it as ornately spectacular and lavish as possible, absolutely no expense was spared.

The large Baroque façade is decorated with columns, cornices and an abundance of carved angels and saints. Théophile Gautier writes that the interior decorations 'make the chapel of the Holy Virgin look like a chorus girl's boudoir'. The elaboration covers every centimetre of the interior: gold and white stucco, a proliferation of green and white marble giving the impression of festoons of damask, and ornate altars.

The finest work of art is Titian's famous *Martyrdom of St Lawrence* (first altar on the left), which alone merits a visit to the church.
Campo dei Gesuiti, Cannaregio. Tel: 041 528 6579. Open: Apr–Oct daily 10am–noon & 4–6pm; Nov–Mar daily 10am–noon & 3–5.30pm. Vaporetto: Nos 41/42 or 51/52 to Fondamente Nuove.

The Ghetto

The word 'ghetto', from the Venetian word *getare*, meaning 'to cast', derives from the foundry which existed in this district centuries ago. The Ghetto was founded in 1516 – the first time a defined area of a city had been allocated for the Jewish community. The name was subsequently used for Jewish enclaves in cities all over the world.

The Ghetto comprised a small island cut off from the rest of the city by wide canals and heavy gateways which were bolted at night. The tight restriction of space forced the Jews to build vertically, hence the tenement blocks – or the 'skyscrapers of Venice' – which you can still see.

Napoleon abolished the gates in 1797, but it was not until 1866 that the Jews were permitted to live where they pleased. Today, only half a dozen Jewish families live in the Ghetto, though others come from elsewhere in the city for the Levantine bread, kosher food, shops, library and the regular services held in a synagogue.

Guided tour of the synagogues

The synagogues are not open on a regular basis, and this tour – given by a highly knowledgeable guide – offers you a rare opportunity to see their richly decorated interiors. There are five synagogues in all, of which you are likely to see three. The most sumptuously decorated are the Levantine, Spanish and the Canton.

Be tempted by the Jewish specialities for sale in the Ghetto

The tour will start with the German Synagogue, above the museum (*see below*). The marble surfaces are made from marble dust – in fact, Jews were originally forbidden to use slabs of marble in their buildings because it was deemed too grand a material for their use.

Tours leave from the Museo Ebraico daily, except Sat, at 30 minutes past the hour from 10.30am to 5.30pm (4.30pm in winter). Admission charge.

Museo Ebraico

This is a small museum devoted mainly to antique ornaments and silverware used in Jewish religious ceremonies. These include Sabbath and Hanukkah lamps, spice boxes, oil lamps and rams' horns blown at New Year and at the end of the Day of Atonement.

Campo Ghetto Nuovo, Cannaregio 2902/b. Tel: 04 171 5359. www.museo ebraico.it. Open: 1 Jun–30 Sept Sun–Fri 10am–7pm; 1 Oct–31 May Sun–Fri 10am–6pm. Closed Sat & Jewish festivals. Admission charge. Vaporetto: Nos 41/42 & 51/52 to Ponte delle Guglie.

Madonna dell'Orto

The lovely Gothic church of Madonna dell'Orto, distinctive for the onion-shaped cupola of its *campanile*, stands in a quiet corner of Cannaregio. Originally dedicated to St Christopher, it acquired its present name through a statue of the *Madonna and Child* discovered in a nearby *orto* (garden). Said to have miraculous powers, the statue was set in the church with the hope that donations would flow in.

This was the first church to be restored after the devastating floods of 1966. This massive project was funded by the British and Italian Art and Archives Rescue Fund, and two years later the ten Tintoretto paintings were restored at the expense of the government.

Façade

The pink brick façade, decorated with a wealth of carvings, is one of the best examples of Venetian Gothic architecture. Statues of the Apostles are set in slanting rows of niches, while the elegant portal, showing the transition between Gothic and Renaissance styles, is crowned by a statue of St Christopher. Flanking the doorway are statues of the Virgin and the angel Gabriel.

Interior

The interior is simple, spacious and serene. Most of the works of art are by Tintoretto, who was a parishioner of the church. The most prominent of these works are the two huge and dramatic canvases either side of the high altar: the *Last Judgement*, and the *Worship of the Golden Calf* with what is believed to be a self-portrait of Tintoretto carrying the calf, fourth from the left. Tintoretto's dramatically

conceived *Presentation of the Virgin in the Temple* hangs above the door of the Capella di San Mauro.

Over the first altar on the right is Cima da Conegliano's masterly depiction of *St John the Baptist and Saints*. Opposite, in the first chapel on the left, Giovanni Bellini's charming little *Madonna and Child* was stolen for a third time and has not found its way back to its slot in the church.

Campo Madonna dell'Orto, Cannaregio. Tel: 041 275 0462. www.chorus venezia.org. Open: Mon–Sat 10am–5pm, Sun 1–5pm. Admission charge. Vaporetto: Nos 41/42 & 51/52 to Madonna dell'Orto.

The façade of the Madonna dell'Orto

Cannaregio

Walk: Cannaregio

This walk takes you to some of the quietest and most remote quarters of the city. The Ghetto and the Church of the Madonna dell'Orto are the cultural highlights.

Allow 1½ hours.

For a map of the route, see p95.

Start at the station and take the Rio Terra Lista di Spagna as far as Campo San Geremia.

1 Church of San Geremia

The church is the resting place of St Lucy of Syracuse, who was removed from the Church of Santa Lucia when it was demolished to make room for the railway station. Her sarcophagus lies in the chapel opposite the entrance.

2 Palazzo Labia

The palace beside the church was built by the wealthy Labia family. The ballroom is decorated with some of Tiepolo's finest frescoes, depicting *The Life of Cleopatra*. At the time of going to press, the palace was closed for lengthy restoration work, with no completion date available (*for information, telephone 041 781 111*).
Continue to the end of the street and cross the bridge.

3 Canale di Cannaregio

Before the Ponte della Libertà was constructed, this was the main entrance into Venice. Today, it is a good area to see everyday Venetian life. There are basic shops and bars, fish and fruit stalls, and tiny *trattorie* serving Venetian food.
Turn left and take the third sottoportego *(alley) marked 'Sinagoghe'. Walk through the Ghetto Vecchio, crossing Campo delle Scuole, and on to Campo Ghetto Nuovo.*

4 Campo Ghetto Nuovo

Despite the name, the 'New Ghetto' is the world's oldest (*see pp97–8*). Only a handful of Jews live here now, but the surroundings still have an ethnic air. Set under symbolic strips of barbed wire, seven evocative bas-reliefs by Arbit Blatas commemorate the Jews who suffered in the Holocaust.
Cross the bridge on the north side of the square, turn right, and follow the fondamenta *until you see an alley marked 'Ospedale'. Turn left here, cross*

over the next bridge, and then turn right along Fondamenta della Sensa.

5 Campo dei Mori

The Mori are the oriental figures carved on the *campo* walls. It is said they were merchants belonging to the Mastelli family, who came to Venice in the 12th century from the Peloponnese (Morea, hence Mori) and lived in Palazzo Mastelli, which once backed on to the square. The house where Tintoretto lived (Casa del Tintoretto) lies along the waterfront (No 3399), just past another turbaned merchant. *Cross the bridge north of the square.*

6 Madonna dell'Orto

This is the most charming Gothic church in Venice (*see pp98–9*). It is full of works of art, many by Tintoretto. The surrounding neighbourhood is quiet, simple and picturesque, with only the occasional barge breaking the silence. *Orto* means 'kitchen garden', and there are still gardens here, albeit small and hidden behind walls. *Follow the canal eastwards, cross the bridge at the end, and walk on to Rio della Sensa. Turn left for Campo dell'Abbazia. Cross the bridge and pass, on your right, the massive brick Misericórdia. Cross another two canals, pass under the passageway, and turn left at Calle della Racchetta (marked 'Racheta'). Walk up to Fondamente Nuove.*

7 Fondamente Nuove

This long, straight quayside was built at the end of the 16th century. From here, boats depart for the outlying islands in the northern lagoon. Across the water, dark cypress trees rise above the cemetery of the Isola di San Michele. *Vaporetto Nos 41/42 & 51/52 will take you back to the station, to San Zaccaria (near San Marco) or (the 41/42) to Murano.*

The iron-nosed statue of Sior Antonio Riota overlooks Campo dei Mori

Santi Apostoli

The site was occupied by some of the first inhabitants of Venice. The church has often been rebuilt, but assumed its present form in the mid-18th century. The *campanile* dates from 1672 and is one of the tallest in Venice. Inside, the highlight is the lovely Renaissance Corner Chapel, thought to have been designed by Mauro Coducci. This contains the tomb of Marco Corner, attributed to Tullio Lombardo, and, above the altar, Tiepolo's *Communion of Santa Lucia* (1748).

Campo Santi Apostoli, Cannaregio.
Tel: 041 523 8297. Open: daily

Ceiling panel in the church of Santi Apostoli frescoed by Fabio Canal

7.30–11.30am & 5–7pm. Vaporetto: No 1 to Ca' d'Oro.

San Giobbe

Standing on a remote square near the Cannaregio Canal, San Giobbe is one of the earliest examples of Renaissance architecture in Venice. The church was begun in 1450 in Gothic style, then completed in the 1470s by Pietro Lombardo. Outstanding features are Lombardo's finely carved Renaissance saints over the portal and, inside the church, his domed chancel and triumphal arch. The great San Giobbe altarpieces by Giovanni Bellini and Carpaccio were removed to the Accademia Galleries when Napoleon suppressed the San Giobbe monastery.

Among the pieces left worth singling out is Antonio Vivarini's delightful triptych of *The Annunciation*, showing in the pose of the figures and the perspective the influence of the Florentine Renaissance. The Cappella Martini (second chapel on the left) was built for a family of silk weavers from Lucca and has a ceiling covered with glazed terracotta reliefs in the style of the Florentine Della Robbia family.

Campo San Giobbe, Cannaregio.
Tel: 041 275 0462. www.chorus venezia.org. Open: Mon–Sat 10am–5pm. Admission charge. Vaporetto: No 41/42 to Crea.

Santa Maria dei Miracoli

It is no wonder that most Venetians want to get married in the Miracoli.

The severe façade of Galleries San Giobbe hides the treasures inside

It is the most exquisite of Venetian churches, frequently likened to a jewel box. Both exterior and interior are decorated and carved with patterns of inlaid multicoloured marble.

The church was built between 1481 and 1489 to enshrine an image of the Virgin that was believed to have miraculous powers. It was designed by Pietro Lombardo and his sons, and the successful blend of Veneto-Byzantine and Renaissance styles is considered the most important work of this leading Venetian architect and sculptor.

No less impressive than the façade, the interior is decorated in grey and coral marble and has an abundance of crisp, classically inspired sculpture. At the east end of the church the balustrade is adorned with Tullio Lombardo's half-figures of St Francis, the Archangel Gabriel, the Virgin, and St Clare. The wooden barrel-vaulted ceiling of the nave is decorated with 50 portraits of saints and prophets.

As in so many churches in Venice, the surfaces are being severely and rapidly corroded by the rising water and salt. Unsympathetic restoration in the past did not stem the damage, but the American Save Venice Organization helped raise more than half a million dollars, and the church has undergone a major restoration programme.

Campo dei Miracoli, Cannaregio. Tel: 041 275 0462. www.chorusvenezia. org. Open: Mon–Sat 10am–5pm, Sun 1–5pm. Admission charge. Vaporetto: Nos 1 & 2 to Rialto.

Castello

Of the six sestieri, *Castello is widely considered to be the most authentically 'Venetian'. Its proximity to the erstwhile shipyards of the Arsenale means it was traditionally a working-class enclave, and the area has retained something of its grittiness over the centuries. However, this – at least comparatively speaking – leafy district is not without its charms: here you can find an amazing cycle of paintings by Carpaccio, a hospital that looks like a wedding cake and one of the most important churches in all the city.*

Arsenale

'A very wreck found drifting in the sea' was how Charles Dickens described the Arsenale in 1844, and not much has changed since then. Seeing the desolate dockyards today, it is hard to believe that this was once the greatest naval base in the world. During the heyday of the Venetian Republic, a workforce of over 16,000 was employed to build, equip and refurbish the great galleys. English author John Evelyn wrote that during the time it took King Henry III of France to eat his dinner on a visit to Venice in 1574, an entire galley was 'built, rigg'd and fitted for launching'.

Today, the 32ha (80-acre) area may appear deserted, but a fascinating range of activities is under way inside.

Entrance to the Arsenale, the naval nerve-centre of the Venetian Republic

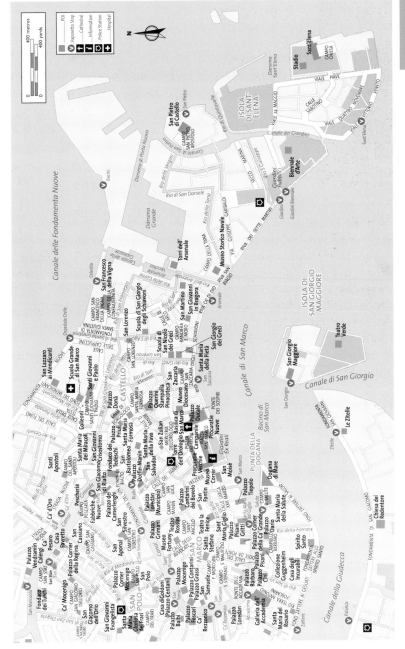

Alongside the navy, which demarcates its area with warning signs, a research centre for avant-garde marine technology has been set up, and the Biennale cultural organisation is doing a magnificent job of refurbishing vast historic structures as theatres and contemporary art exhibition venues. The **Museo Storico Navale** (Naval History Museum; *see p109*) houses a 15th-century galley discovered in the lagoon.

The word *arsenale* derives from the Arabic *darsina'a*, meaning a house of industry or a workshop. Venice's Arsenale was the first to be constructed and gave its name to shipyards all over the world.

Visitors can get an excellent sense of the extent of the Arsenale by taking the No 41/42 *vaporetto* via San Pietro circling its eastern reaches.

Heralding the great shipyard (*see pp116–17*) is the triumphal walled gateway, one of the earliest pieces of Renaissance architecture in Venice.

The towering Gothic church dominates Campo Santi Giovanni e Paolo

Campo Santi Giovanni e Paolo

More familiarly known as Campo San Zanipolo, this ceremonial square is overlooked by the great Gothic church from which it takes its name. The northern side is flanked by the sumptuous marble façade of the Scuola Grande di San Marco. The free-standing equestrian monument of the great military leader Bartolomeo Colleoni, by Verrocchio, is one of the most famous pieces of early Renaissance sculpture.

John Ruskin was one of many art historians who heaped praise on the statue: 'I do not believe that there is a more glorious work of sculpture existing in the world.'

The fabulously rich and successful *condottiere* Bartolomeo Colleoni offered a large part of his fortune to the Venetian Republic on condition that when he died a monument be erected to him 'in front of San Marco'. No other monument had graced the Piazza, so rather than break with tradition, the Senate, in its characteristically crafty way, found a loophole to secure the legacy. Since the *condottiere* had not specified the Basilica di San Marco, they placed him instead in front of the Scuola Grande di San Marco.

Andrea Verrocchio, who designed the monument, died in the course of its construction, and the work was completed by the Venetian sculptor Alessandro Leopardi, whose signature can be seen on one of the horse's straps.

Scuola Grande di San Marco

The headquarters of the Scuola was built between 1485 and 1495 to replace the first building, which had been destroyed by fire. Since the beginning of the 19th century, it has been the Ospedale Civile (Civic Hospital).

Its finest features are the richly decorated asymmetrical façade and the *trompe-l'œil* arcades, designed by Pietro Lombardo with his sons and Giovanni Buora. These were recently restored to their former glory by Save Venice. The building was completed in 1495 by Mauro Coducci. Wander through the cavernous entrance hall, all the way through to the lagoon edge. The ancient buildings and the ultra-modern hospital wings make a striking contrast.

Museo Diocesano d'Arte Sacra (Diocesan Museum of Sacred Art)

Only a stone's throw from the madding crowds in San Marco, the cloister of the Convent of Sant'Apollonia is remarkably peaceful. As indeed it wishes to be; a plaque beside the portal reads: *Conoscete Voi il chiostro di S. Apollonia?… Un piccolo chiostro segreto* (Do you know the cloister of S.

Diocesan Museum of Sacred Art

Apollonia?... A little secret cloister). Apart from being beautiful and charming, it is the only Romanesque cloister in Venice. Scattered round the walls are ornamental fragments of capitals, sarcophagi and gravestones of Roman and Byzantine origin, many of them pilfered from Constantinople.

The museum beyond the cloister houses a collection of paintings, illustrated manuscripts, crucifixes, gold and silverware taken from deconsecrated and abandoned churches or removed from those which are temporarily closed. Paintings include works by Palma il Giovane and Luca Giordano, and among the church treasures is a fine 16th-century lacquered-wood and crystal tabernacle.

Should you show sufficient interest in the exhibits, the custodian will happily give you a tour, but only in Italian. Alternatively, there are sheets in English detailing the contents of the museum.

Sant'Apollonia, Ponte della Canonica, Castello. Tel: 041 522 9166. www.veneziaubc.org. Open: daily 10am–6pm. Admission charge. Vaporetto: Nos 1, 2, 41/42 & 51/52 to San Zaccaria.

Museo della Fondazione Querini Stampalia (Museum of the Querini Stampalia Foundation)

Centuries ago, the Querini family ruled the Greek island of Stampalia, hence the double-barrelled name of their 16th-century Venetian palace. In 1869, Giovanni, the last of the Querinis, bequeathed the palace and his Venetian paintings and prints, spanning 400 years of Venetian art, to the city.

Four hundred years of Venetian art features at the Museum of the Querini Stampalia Foundation

The artists include Giovanni Bellini, Tiepolo, Longhi and Palma il Vecchio. A fascinating series by Gabriele Bella, *Scenes from Venetian Public Life*, showing 18th-century festive scenes, and group portraits by the prolific Pietro Longhi, immediately recognisable by their doll-like figures, are also on show. The library houses over 230,000 books. The palace has been splendidly refurbished and there have also been some modern additions by the architect Carlo Scarpa, including a Japanese-style bridge and garden. It is regularly the venue of exhibitions.

Realistic displays at the Naval History Museum

Palazzo Querini Stampalia, Campo SM Formosa, Castello. Tel: 041 271 1411. http://querinistampalia.it. Open: Tue–Sun 10am–7pm (until 10pm on Fri & Sat). Closed: Mon. Admission charge. Vaporetto: Nos 1, 2, 41/42 & 51/52 to San Zaccaria.

Museo Storico Navale (Naval History Museum)

This is a fascinating museum even for non-maritime enthusiasts. A rare bonus is the labelling, which is in English as well as Italian. The exhibits span several centuries and include spoils from Venetian sea victories and models of Venetian (and other) ships and boats. Among these are the original gondolas (equipped with a *felze*, or cabin) and a reconstruction of the famous Bucintoro, the carved and gilded state barge used by the doge. The original was stripped of all its ornamentation by

Napoleon, who also melted down cannons and bronzes of Venetian vessels for the famous column in the Place Vendôme in Paris in celebration of the French Revolution.

The most recent exhibits, displayed on the ground floor, are the 'human torpedoes' used in World War II.

Campo San Biagio, Arsenale, Castello. Tel: 041 244 1399. Open: Mon–Fri 8.45am–1.30pm, Sat 8.45am–1pm. Admission charge. Vaporetto: No 1 to Arsenale.

Ospedaletto (Santa Maria dei Derelitti)

The Ospedaletto complex comprises the Church of Santa Maria dei Derelitti and the hospice of Santi Giovanni e Paolo, which is now in use as an old people's home.

The church (1662–74) was designed by Baldassare Longhena and the façade (*Cont. on p112*)

Walk: Castello

This walk takes you from the panoramic Riva degli Schiavoni promenade to the contrastingly quiet squares, streets and churches of Castello.

Allow 2 hours, excluding sights.

Start at Riva degli Schiavoni. Sixty metres (197ft) beyond the Danieli Hotel, turn left under the passageway.

1 Campo San Zaccaria

This quiet *campo* is flanked by the lovely façade of the Church of San Zaccaria (*see pp118–20*). The Benedictine convent adjoining the church was notorious for the promiscuous behaviour of its nuns. *Turn right into Campo San Provolo and under the* sottoportico *for Fondamenta dell'Osmarin. At the end of the canal, cross the two bridges.*

2 San Giorgio dei Greci

Built in 1530, long after a Greek colony was established in Venice, the Church of San Giorgio dei Greci is still used as a place of worship by the Greek Orthodox community. The most distinctive exterior feature is the tilting *campanile. From the bridge, walk east along an alley to join the Salizzada dei Greci. At the end, cross the bridge and turn left along*

the canal to the Scuola di San Giorgio degli Schiavoni (see pp120–21). Cross the bridge close to the scuola, turn right, and just before a portico, turn left down Calle San Lorenzo.

3 Church of San Lorenzo

San Lorenzo claims to be the burial place of Marco Polo. The tomb, if it existed, was lost when the church was rebuilt in 1592. The church has fallen into a state of disrepair.
Cross over the Rio di San Lorenzo and zigzag left and right into Borgoloco San Lorenzo. Cross over the next canal, and at the end of the street turn right.

4 Campo Santa Maria Formosa

Once the scene of bullfights and open-air theatre, this large rambling square is flanked by some very fine *palazzi* and is dominated by Mauro Coducci's Church of Santa Maria Formosa (*see p115*). *Take the narrow Calle Lunga Santa Maria Formosa eastwards. Turn left at the third street, cross a canal and* continue north for Campo Santi Giovanni e Paolo.

5 Campo Santi Giovanni e Paolo

Sit at one of the cafés to savour the wealth of architecture and sculpture around you (*see also pp106–7 & pp113–14*). The great Church of Santi Giovanni e Paolo (San Zanipolo) towers over the square. The elaborately decorated Renaissance Scuola Grande di San Marco beside it is now the city hospital.

Cross the bridge from the campo, *and follow the narrow streets to the Miracoli in adjacent Cannaregio (*see pp102–3*). Cross the bridge at the side of the church into Campo Santa Maria Nova and follow the streets to the Salizzada San*

Canciano. Turn left here to Campiello Flaminio and cross the bridge.

6 Church of San Giovanni Crisostomo

Squashed into a little square north of the Rialto, this was Coducci's last work, built at the turn of the 15th century. The interior is intimate and richly decorated. The finest paintings are Giovanni Bellini's *St Jerome with Saints Christopher and Augustine* and Sebastiano del Piombo's *St John Chrysostom and Six Saints*.

The church is open Mon–Sat 10am–5pm, Sun & public holidays 1–5pm. Follow the streets to the Rialto, where you can pick up a waterbus in either direction.

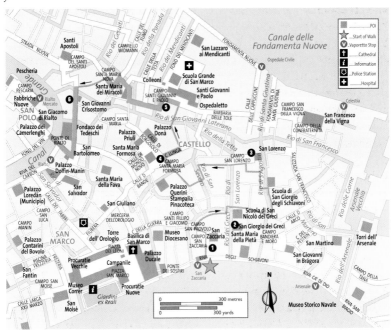

is Baroque at its most grotesque. The neighbouring hospital was set up as a charitable institution to care for the sick and to educate orphan girls in religion and music. The frescoed Sala della Musica, where they performed, is now open to the public.
Calle Barbaria delle Tole, Castello. Tel: 041 271 9012. Open: Sat–Sun 3–6pm. Vaporetto: Nos 41/42 & 51/52 to Ospedale Civile.

San Francesco della Vigna
The original 13th-century church stood on the site of a cultivated vineyard – hence the name 'della Vigna'. The 'new' Franciscan church was begun by Sansovino in 1534, and the imposing façade, with statues of St Paul and Moses, was added between 1562 and 1572 to a design by Andrea Palladio.

The interior, in the form of a Latin cross with a single nave, is spacious and perfectly proportioned. It is also rich in works of art, including some very fine sculpture by Alessandro Vittoria, the most prolific and talented sculptor of 16th-century Venice, and by the Lombardo family and workshop.

The most noteworthy paintings are the *Holy Family with Saints* by Veronese (fifth chapel on the left), Antonio da Negroponte's delightful *Virgin and Child* (right transept) and, in the Cappella Santa close to the beautiful 15th-century cloisters, Giovanni Bellini's compelling *Madonna and Child with Saints.*

Doge Andrea Gritti, who is said to have died from a surfeit of eels, is buried in the chancel.
Campo della Confraternità, Castello, 2786. Tel: 041 520 6102. Open: daily 8am–12.30pm & 3–7pm. Vaporetto: Nos 41/41 & 51/52 to Celestia.

San Giovanni in Bragora
The simple Gothic Church of San Giovanni in Bragora stands on a very quiet square, a stone's throw from the busy Riva degli Schiavoni.

The interior is strong on early Renaissance art. The church's greatest treasure is Cima da Conegliano's *Baptism of Christ* (1492–5), which lies behind the altar. Fabulously improved by restoration, the painting shows the figures set against the landscape of the artist's native Veneto region.

In the chapel to the left of the chancel, Bartolomeo Vivarini's triptych of *Madonna and Child with St John and St Andrew* was painted only 14 years before Cima's *Baptism of Christ*, yet the Byzantine-influenced gold background, the flat space and the posed figures give the impression it was produced long before Cima's masterpiece.

There are several works by Alvise Vivarini, Bartolomeo's nephew, the finest of which is the forward-looking *Resurrection* (1498) on the left of the sacristy door. Antonio Vivaldi was a parishioner here and was baptised at the 15th-century font.
Campo Bandiera e Moro, Castello. Tel: 041 270 2464. Open: Mon–Sat

Castello

9–11am & 3.30–5.30pm. Vaporetto: No 1 to Arsenale.

Santi Giovanni e Paolo

The Basilica of Santi Giovanni e Paolo (also known to older Venetians as San Zanipolo) is a synthesis of the glories of Venice. It similtaneously functions as one of the two great Gothic churches in the city, as the Pantheon of the Doges and as a museum of Gothic and Renaissance Venetian funerary sculpture. It also boasts important works by Venetian painters.

Façade

The soaring Gothic edifice is the dominant feature of northern Castello. Built as a Dominican friary in the 13th century, it was dedicated to two brother saints (John and Paul)

martyred in Rome in the 4th century. The most notable feature of its unfinished brick façade is the bold Renaissance porch, attributed to Bartolomeo Bon. Finished in 1463, and decorated with carvings, it is one of the very earliest Renaissance architectural features in Venice.

Interior

The first impression is of monumental austerity, appropriate to the character both of the doges and the Dominican order. The church, built in the form of a Latin Cross, ends with five polygonal apses and is supported by ten massive columns with pointed arcades and cross

PLAN OF SANTI GIOVANNI E PAOLO

1 Monument to Doge Giovanni Mocenigo
2 Monument to Pietro Mocenigo
3 Monument to Marcantonio Bragadin
4 Polyptych of St Vincent Ferrer by Giovanni Bellini
5 Cappella della Madonna della Pace
6 Cappella di San Domenico
7 *Christ Bearing the Cross* by Alvise Vivarini and *Coronation of the Virgin* by Cima da Conegliano
8 Monument to the *condottiere* Brisighella
9 Monument to Michele Morosini
10 Monument to Doge Leonardo Loredan
11 Monument to Andrea Vendramin
12 Monument to Marco Corner
13 Monuments to Giovanni Dolfin and Jacopo Cavalli
14 Bronze statue of Doge Sebastiano Venier
15 Cappella del Rosario
16 Sacristy
17 Monument to Pasquale Malipiero
18 Monument to Tommaso Mocenigo
19 Monument to Nicolò Marcello

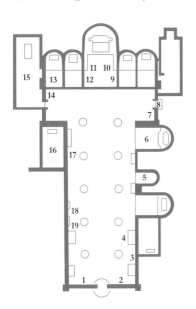

vaulting – the whole structure being stabilised by a lattice of tie beams.

Monuments

More than 20 funeral monuments are hard to digest in one go, so those selected here are seven of the finest, listed in chronological order. This will involve some inconvenient criss-crossing of the basilica but will enable you to follow the development of Venetian sculpture from Gothic to High Renaissance. The church has the finest examples in Venice of works by the Lombardo family: Pietro (c.1435–1515) and his sons, Tullio (1455–1532) and Antonio (1458–1516). The Lombardi became the leading sculptors of the Renaissance period in Venice.

The following monuments are located as shown on the plan (*see p113*):

12 (Chancel): the monument to Doge Marco Corner (d.1368) is a Gothic piece by Tuscan sculptor Nino Pisano.

9 (Chancel): the monument to Doge Michele Morosini (d.1382) was described by John Ruskin as 'the richest monument of the Gothic period in Venice'.

18 (North Aisle): the monument to Doge Tommaso Mocenigo (d.1423), by Florentine sculptors working in Venice, is a transitional work with both Gothic and Renaissance elements.

17 (North Aisle): the monument to Doge Pasquale Malipiero (d.1462) by Pietro Lombardo is Renaissance in style but not entirely free of Gothic influence.

19 (North Aisle): the monument to Doge Nicolò Marcello (d.1474) by

Pietro Lombardo is more evidently classical, as shown, for instance, by the natural composure of the Virgin in the lunette.

11 (Chancel): the monument to Doge Andrea Vendramin (d.1478), a High Renaissance masterpiece, is completely classical in conception. Note the figures which are perfectly balanced and composed. The monument was designed by Pietro Lombardo and carved by Tullio.

2 (West Wall): the monument to Doge Pietro Mocenigo (d.1476) is also by Pietro Lombardo. It was completed in 1481 and characterises the climax of the Venetian High Renaissance.

Paintings

Two great works of art are Giovanni Bellini's magnificent *St Vincent Ferrer* polyptych, over the second altar, south aisle (**4**), and G B Piazzetta's *Glory of St Dominic* (1727), on the ceiling of the Cappella di San Domenico (**6**). The spiralling composition and startling *trompe-l'œil* effects show how Piazzetta influenced Tiepolo. The works in the Cappella del Rosario (**15**) were destroyed by fire in 1867. The chapel was restored and now has ceiling paintings by Veronese.

Campo Santi Giovanni e Paolo, Castello. Tel: 041 523 5913. www.basilicasantigiovanniepaolo.it. Open: Mon–Sat 9am–6pm & Sun noon–6pm. Admission charge. Vaporetto: Nos 41/42 & 51/52 to Ospedale Civile, or Nos 1 & 2 to Rialto.

Santa Maria Formosa

With its swelling, cream-coloured apses, the church is the dominant feature of the rambling Campo Santa Maria Formosa. The ancient church that stood here was rebuilt in 1492 to a design by Mauro Coducci. The grotesque mask at the foot of the *campanile* is one of the many lavish Baroque details.

Inside the church, the *pièce de résistance* is Palma il Vecchio's polyptych of *Santa Barbara and Saints*. Generally regarded as the artist's finest work – and looking particularly splendid after its complete restoration – the altarpiece shows a serene, majestic and amply endowed St Barbara, with saints either side and a *pietà* above. St Barbara was the patron saint of soldiers, and it was the Confraternity of the Bombardiers who commissioned the painting for their chapel. The 16th-century art critic Giorgio Vasari described the work as 'a picture which in its completeness, dignity, decorative feeling and depth of colour may be ranked with the great masterpieces of the Venetian school'.

The other masterpiece – although it is inevitably upstaged by the Palma il Vecchio – is Bartolomeo Vivarini's *Triptych of the Madonna of the Misericordia* (1473), which was financed by the congregation of the church and is even said to feature some of the parishioners.

Campo Santa Maria Formosa, Castello. Tel: 041 275 0462. www.chorusvenezia. org. Open: Mon–Sat 10am–5pm. Admission charge. Vaporetto: Nos 1 & 2 to Rialto.

Santa Barbara and Saints (detail) by Palma il Vecchio, Santa Maria Formosa

San Pietro di Castello

It is hard to believe that this church, standing on a remote grassy *campo* of eastern Venice, was for many years the religious centre of the city. It was built in the late 16th century and, until 1807, when the bishop's see was transferred to the Basilica of San Marco, this was the cathedral of Venice. The church maintains its dignity but the area

(*Cont. on p118*)

Walk: Arsenale and Biennale

A leisurely stroll takes you eastwards, through the old shipyards of the great maritime republic to the largest park in the city.

Allow a couple of hours for the round trip.

Start at the San Zaccaria vaporetto *stop and walk eastwards along the quayside.*

1 Riva degli Schiavoni
This curving promenade is named after the Dalmatian merchants who used to moor their boats and barges here. *Continue to just beyond the third bridge.*

2 La Pietà
Known as Vivaldi's church, it was here that the composer directed concerts and gave violin lessons to orphan girls. Little survives of the original building, but if it is open (*Thur–Sun 10am–5pm*), step inside to admire Tiepolo's *Triumph of Faith*, frescoed on the ceiling. For information about concerts, *telephone 041 523 7395. Take the alley immediately after the church, turn right at the Hotel Bisanzio and cross the next bridge.*

3 Campo Bandiera e Moro
This small, unassuming square provides a quiet contrast to the frenzy of the

waterfront just a stone's throw away. The delightful Gothic Church of San Giovanni in Bragora (*see pp112–13*) stands on the far side, a plaque on the wall recording Vivaldi's baptism here. *Take the street to the left of the church, then fork left for Calle del Pestrin. Turn right at the end, cross the bridge and pass San Martino Church on your right.*

4 Campo dell'Arsenale
The café here is a convenient spot to sit and contemplate the sturdy watchtowers protecting the lagoon entrance to the Arsenale and the handsome gateway of the shipyard. Here, the large winged lion of St Mark now conceals the inapt message in his book: *Pax Tibi Marce, Evangelista meus* (Peace be with you Mark, my Evangelist). In a niche beside the archway, a plaque records Dante's reference to the Arsenale in *The Divine Comedy*. The writer came here in 1306 and 1321, and the scene of frenzied activity left a lasting impression.

Cross the bridge and turn right towards the waterfront. Turn left at the end, passing the Museo Storico Navale (see p109), and cross Rio della Tana.

5 Riva dei Sette Martiri

The Sette Martiri (seven martyrs) refers to the Venetian women who were shot in World War II. A large bronze commemorative statue can be seen on the steps along the quay when the tide is not too high. It is a great place for boat-spotting: liners, ferries, sailing boats, speedboats, *vaporetti*, tugs and barges all ply the waters here.

6 Giardini Pubblici/Biennale

A stroll through the public gardens will bring you to the permanent pavilions of the Biennale. If it is summer in an odd-numbered year, the place will be swarming with Italian and foreign enthusiasts of modern art who have come to see the exhibitions in the pavilions. Some of the pavilions are works of art in themselves.

7 Parco delle Rimembranze

You can take *vaporetti* Nos 1 and 2 from the Giardini and Giardini Biennale landing stages, or continue your stroll along the quayside as far as the Parco delle Rimembranze. This is a favourite spot for Venetian joggers. *Vaporetto* No 1 calls at Sant'Elena, and a seat on the right-hand side will give fine views of the quaysides as the waterbus weaves its way back to San Marco.

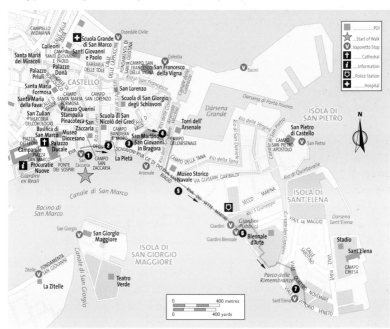

San Pietro di Castello

surrounding it is comparatively humble, with washing strung across the streets and under the arches of the abandoned Patriarchal Palace cloister.

The church has no outstanding works of art, but a printed sheet (translated into English) gives a few details of the paintings, chapels and sculpture.

Detached from the church on the square stands Coducci's elegant, though now leaning, *campanile*. This was the first bell tower in Venice to be faced in white Istrian stone.

Isola di San Pietro. Tel: 041 275 0462. www.chorusvenezia.org. Open: Mon–Sat 10am–5pm. Admission charge. Vaporetto: No 1 to Giardini, 2 to Giardini Biennale or 41/42 & 51/52 to San Pietro.

San Zaccaria

Founded in the 9th century, the Church of San Zaccaria was rebuilt between 1458 and 1515. The façade is one of the most beautiful examples of early Venetian Renaissance architecture. Although begun by Antonio Gambello in Gothic style, the first storey and upwards were designed and completed by Mauro Coducci. The interior is largely Gothic in layout but Renaissance in its decoration. The greatest treasure is Giovanni Bellini's glorious *Madonna and Child with Saints*, above the second altarpiece on the left. Napoleon admired the painting so much that he took it off with him in 1797 to Paris, where he kept it for 20 years. To really appreciate the rich colours you need to put coins in the lighting box.

Every year at Easter the doge and his entourage would visit this church for vespers. The adjoining convent was occupied by nuns who threw wild parties for young patricians, entertained their lovers and generally

The charming façade of San Zaccaria blends Renaissance with flamboyant Gothic

St Augustine in his Study, by Carpaccio, in the Scuola di San Giorgio degli Schiavoni

created scandal throughout the city. Given that many were sent here against their will, particularly if their fathers couldn't, or wouldn't, fork out for a dowry, it is perhaps not surprising that they were anything but devout.

Chapel of St Athanasius

This was the central part of the church, made into a chapel in 1595. It is flanked by finely carved choirstalls and hung with poorly lit paintings of Venetian masters.

Chapel of San Tarasio

This was the chancel of the old church. The waterlogged crypt under the chapel is the oldest part, and contains the relics of eight doges who ruled from 836 to 1172. The vault is decorated with

15th-century frescoes which are the earliest works of the Florentine master Andrea del Castagno. On the altar and walls there are three finely carved and gilded late Gothic altarpieces.

Campo San Zaccaria, Castello.
Tel: 041 522 1257.
Open: Mon–Sat 10am–noon &
4–6pm, Sun and public holidays
4–6pm. Admission charge to chapels
and crypt. Vaporetto: any to
San Zaccaria.

Scuola di San Giorgio degli Schiavoni

The Scuola was founded in 1451 by Dalmatians (hence Schiavoni, or Slavs) to protect their community in Venice. With the funds it had accumulated through Dalmatian trading in Venice, the Scuola was able to commission Vittore Carpaccio – then at the height of his career – to decorate the upper hall. The paintings were created between 1502 and 1509 in the upper hall, then transferred to the ground level when the Scuola was reconstructed in 1552. The room itself hardly does justice to the exquisite frieze of paintings. To Henry James it was a 'shabby little chapel' but also 'a palace of art'.

The scenes are richly coloured and vivid, combining fantasy with meticulously observed detail. Besides being fine works of art, they also provide a fascinating documentation of Venetian life. All, apart from two, depict episodes from the lives of three Dalmatian saints: St George (who the Dalmatians claimed was a Dalmatian), St Tryphon and St Jerome. If you start on the left wall and go clockwise, skipping the altarpiece of *The Virgin and Child* by Carpaccio's son, the scenes are as follows: *St George Killing the Dragon, The Triumph of St George, St George Baptising the Heathen King and Queen, St Tryphon before the Emperor Gordianus, The Agony in the Garden, The Calling of St Matthew, St Jerome Leading his Lion into a Monastery, The Funeral of St Jerome* and *St Augustine in his Study.* The last, rendered in meticulous detail, is the most celebrated painting of the cycle. St Augustine is sitting in his Venetian study, writing a letter to St Jerome, when he receives a vision of the saint's death.

Calle Furlani, Castello. Tel: 041 522 8828. Open: Mon 2.45–6pm, Tue–Sat 9am–1pm & 2.45–6pm, Sun 9am–1pm. Admission charge. Vaporetto: any to San Zaccaria.

Scuola di San Nicolò dei Greci

The scuola, designed by Baldassare Longhena in 1678, houses the **Museo Dipinti Sacri Bizanti** (Museum of Sacred Byzantine Art). The Byzantine and post-Byzantine icons date from the 15th to 18th centuries, many of them produced by the Greeks living in Venice at the time.

Ponte dei Greci, Castello, near the Church of San Giorgio dei Greci. Tel: 041 522 6581. Open: daily 9am–5pm (ticket office closes 30 mins earlier). Admission charge. Vaporetto: Nos 1, 2, 42/42 & 51/52 to San Zaccaria.

The Scuola di San Giorgio degli Schiavoni is home to an exquisite cycle of paintings by Carpaccio

Venice environs

The islands surrounding the main city centre are ideal for getting away from the hordes crowding the main sights in town. Though not as jam-packed with architectural and artistic treasures, there is still much to see and to do: the Giudecca has a cornucopia of Palladian churches, Murano and Burano are showcases for the traditional arts of glass-blowing and lacemaking, while Lido has kilometres of beaches for you to lie back and relax or take a bracing seaside stroll (see also map pp22–3).

THE VENETIAN LAGOON
Isola della Giudecca

When Michelangelo fled from Florence in 1529, proclaimed a rebel and deserter, he made the gently curving island known as Spinalunga (Long Spine) his first retreat. In those days it was a pleasure ground of villas, with gardens running down to the lagoon. The fall of the Venetian Republic spelled the gradual decline of this green oasis. Today, Spinalunga is a suburb of Venice made up of interconnecting islets and tightly packed apartments. While it may lack the splendour of Venice 'proper', it has a quiet charm of its own and offers splendid views of the city across the Canale della Giudecca (Giudecca Canal).

The name 'Giudecca' is probably derived from the word *giudicati*, meaning 'judged', for this is where the turbulent nobles of the city were banished. A less likely theory is that the word comes from *giudei*, meaning Jews.

Palladio's churches

The temple-fronted Redentore Church is the main draw of the island and the dominant feature of its waterfront. Palladio's other church, or one thought to be designed from his plans, is the Zitelle at the eastern end of the island. In the 16th century, the adjoining buildings were established as a home for spinsters. Today, the complex assumes a very different role as the city's most up-to-date congress and cultural centre.

The quaysides and the *calli*

On sunny days, the island invites strolling, either alongside the canals, where the fishing community still thrives, or along the main *fondamenta* skirting the Giudecca Canal. It is worth wandering down the dark *sotoportegi* and *calli* (alleys) behind the quayside for the unexpectedness of the bright modern housing. Several former factory sites have been converted into elegant residences with gardens, and the island has been brightened up considerably.

Redentore

Palladio's Redentore Church was built between 1577 and 1592, in thanksgiving for the deliverance of the city from the plague of 1576, which took nearly 50,000 lives.

It stands on the waterfront of the island of Giudecca, and every year on the third Sunday of July, the doge visited the church by crossing a pontoon of boats over the Giudecca Canal. The annual Feast of the Redentore (*see pp16–17*) still celebrates the event.

The church's great dome and white classical façade, brought to life by the play of water and light, make it one of Venice's most conspicuous landmarks. After the elaborate interiors of many Venetian churches, the characteristically Palladian plain stone and whitewashed stucco, unencumbered by colour or

The Venetian lagoon

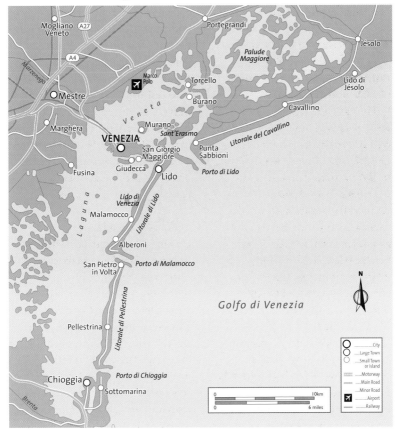

marble, strikes one as refreshingly simple and sober.

The sacristy has the only paintings of note, which include Alvise Vivarini's *Madonna in Adoration of the Child and Two Angels* and a *Baptism of Christ*, attributed to Veronese.

Campo Redentore, Giudecca. Tel: 041 275 0462. www.chorusvenezia. org. Open: Mon–Sat 10am–5pm, Sun 1–5pm. Admission charge. Vaporetto: Nos 2 & 41/42 to Redentore.

Le Zitelle

The Church of Santa Maria della Presentazione, more familiarly called Le Zitelle (the Spinsters), was built according to a Palladian design in 1582–6. Standing on the Giudecca waterfront, with fine views of San Marco, it has a simple façade with a large dome and two side bell towers.

An adjoining hospice was founded for spinsters 'to free them from the dangers of eternal damnation'. The women were taught the art of lacemaking, and became known for their fine *punto in aria* stitchwork. Today, the complex serves as a conference and congress centre, though the church has been preserved as it was.

Fondamenta delle Zitelle, Giudecca. Tel: 04 192 4933. Open: Fri & Sat 3.30–6.30pm. Admission charge. Vaporetto: Nos 2 & 41/42 to Zitelle.

Giudecca is reached via Vaporetto Nos 2 & 41/42.

San Giorgio Maggiore

It is a faint shimmering, airy, watery pink; the bright sea-light seems to flush with it and the pale whitish-green of lagoon and canal to drink it in.

Henry James of the island of San Giorgio Maggiore, *Italian Hours*, 1899.

Seen across the water from San Marco, the island of San Giorgio Maggiore, made up of monastery, church and *campanile*, is one of the most familiar perspectives of Venice. In ancient times, when it was called the Island of Cypresses, vegetable gardens and vineyards flourished here. The island's first monastery was founded by the Benedictines in 982, but rebuilt twice: once in the 13th century after an earthquake, and again in the 15th century.

By the early 17th century, the monastery had become, according to a 16th-century traveller, 'the fairest and

A statue adorning Giudecca's Redentore Church

PALLADIO

One of the most influential figures in Western architecture, Andrea Palladio was an exponent of strict classical form. He aimed to recapture the spirit of ancient Roman buildings, and the hallmarks of his architecture are temple fronts, harmonic proportions and cool, rational beauty. His only churches are to be found in Venice, the finest examples being the Redentore and San Giorgio Maggiore. Palladio was born in Padua, became a student of ancient Roman architecture, and from 1550 designed palaces, villas and churches. The city of Vicenza was almost completely rebuilt after his designs, and there are Palladian villas around Vicenza and along the Brenta Canal.

richest without comparison in all Venice'. A centre of learning, it was also used as a residence for eminent guests, such as Cosimo de' Medici, in 1433 when he was exiled from Florence.

In 1808, Napoleon suppressed the monastery, and all its works of art were dispersed. Under the Austrians, the buildings became barracks, transformed out of recognition. It took another century for the buildings on the island to be restored to their former state.

Church of San Giorgio Maggiore

The Church of San Giorgio Maggiore was built between 1565 and 1576 by the great Italian architect Andrea Palladio. Modelled on the classical style of ancient Rome, it is unsurpassed in its cool, rational beauty. The light, white and grey interior, with the minimum of décor and all-encompassing dome, conveys a wonderful feeling of space and solemnity.

Campanile Access to the *campanile* is well marked from the church. This square brick tower was rebuilt in 1791 after the belfry collapsed. A monk will take you up in the lift for a panorama as stunning as that from the *campanile* in San Marco. The view encompasses city and surroundings; on a clear day, it stretches as far as the Alps. *Admission charge.*

Choir The wooden stalls are decorated with beautifully carved scenes from the life of St Benedict, dating from the late 16th century.

Works of art Coins for the lighting boxes are essential to see the main works of art. Jacopo Bassano's *Nativity* shows a dramatic use of chiaroscuro, depicting a night scene where the infant Jesus is bathed in dazzling light.

Decorating the chancel walls, Tintoretto's *Last Supper* and *Gathering of the Manna* are both immensely powerful works of art, executed when the artist was approaching 80 years of age. The Cappella dei Morti (turn right from the choir) contains Tintoretto's very last painting, *The Deposition*, finished by his son Domenico.

The same chapel has a photograph of Carpaccio's *St George and the Dragon* – the original is locked away. The late 16th-century sculpture by Gerolamo Campagna on the main altar represents the Holy Trinity. The golden globe is

(*Cont. on p128*)

Tour: The Circle Line

This scenic tour on waterbus No 42 takes you along the periphery of Venice (for the route, see map on pp22–3*).*

Allow 1½ hours, including change of boats at Fondamente Nuove.

Start at the No 42 landing stage at San Zaccaria on Riva degli Schiavoni. Be sure to take a boat going in a clockwise direction. You can, of course, alight at any stop en route, then pick up another No 42 (the service runs every 20 minutes during the daytime), but bear in mind that unless you have a travel card this costs a good deal more than staying put on the vaporetto.

1 San Giorgio Maggiore

The shimmering island that the crowds admire from the Piazzetta comes into focus as the *vaporetto* steams across the Bacino di San Marco and heads for the Giudecca Canal (*see pp125 & 128* for Palladio's church and monastery).

2 Giudecca

From the left-hand side of the boat, you can see all the main landmarks of Giudecca. The first church you pass is the Zitelle, said to have been designed by Palladio. However, Giudecca's main monument is Redentore Church (*see*

pp123–4), designed by Palladio, and located close to the next landing stage.

3 Zattere

Across the water, the sun-baked promenade is dotted with open-air cafes, not to mention the prominent church at Gesuati (*see p86*).

4 Molino Stucky

Towards the far end of Giudecca is the huge neo-Gothic structure of the Molino Stucky. This was built in 1895 as a flour mill for Giovanni Stucky, a Swiss industrialist. Stucky was murdered by one of his workers in 1910. However, the mill carried on working until 1954. It is now a luxury Hilton hotel and conference centre.

5 Stazione Marittima

The docklands were first established in the late 1800s and early 1900s. As the boat steams past dockland buildings, wharfs and – nearing the train station – rusting rolling stock, you will be reminded that Venice is not entirely a visual feast.

6 Canale di Cannaregio

Beyond Piazzale Roma and the station, the boat takes in a small stretch of the Grand Canal, then turns left up the Canale di Cannaregio. For those visiting Venice from the mainland before the bridge was built, this wide

The San Giorgio Maggiore is best viewed by boat

canal was the first introduction to the city. Flanking the canal were large palaces with gardens – some of which still exist.

At the end of the canal, where it meets the lagoon, are the elegant buildings of the old abattoir that have now been converted into premises for the university.

7 Fondamente Nuove

The boat skirts northern Venice and stops at Fondamente Nuove. Unless you want to continue to the island of Murano, disembark here and change to a No 42 *vaporetto* returning from Murano and going to San Marco (the landing stages are well marked).

8 Arsenale

The *vaporetto* now skirts the fortified walls of what was once the most important shipyard in the Mediterranean (*see pp104 & 106*). Interspersing the cranes are the buildings where the great galleys were built and fitted out. Round the corner are the castellated towers that mark the grandiose entrance of the shipyard.

9 Grande Finale

As the boat rounds the quiet easternmost corner of Venice, it veers towards Riva degli Schiavoni, affording a spectacular panorama of three great sights of Venice: the island of San Giorgio Maggiore, the Church of the Salute and the splendid palace façades on the Castello/San Marco waterfront.

surmounted by God the Father and supported by the four Evangelists.

Fondazione Giorgio Cini

Thanks to Count Vittorio Cini, the centre has reverted to its original function as a centre of learning. It was bought by the Foundation Giorgio Cini in 1951, restored to its former state and now serves as a foundation for the study of Venetian civilisation.

On a visit to the monastery, you can see Palladio's Cloister of the Cypresses and the refectory (now used as a conference hall), and Longhena's library and double staircase. There is a small café on the eastern side of the island.

Church of San Giorgio Maggiore.
Tel: 041 522 7827. Open: daily
9am–12.30pm & 2.30–4.30pm (later in summer). No sightseeing during services.
Admission charge to campanile *only.*
To visit the Fondazione, call 041 5240119 or visit www.cini.it for guided visits Sat & Sun 10am–4pm every half hour.
Admission charge. Vaporetto: No 2 to San Giorgio.

The Lido

Extending along the mouth of the lagoon, the Lido is an 11km (7-mile) strip of shore which forms a protective barrier between Venice and the sea. The original Lido, it gave its name to bathing establishments all over the world.

Prior to the late 19th-century development, the Lido was no more than an empty spit of sand providing a getaway haven for 19th-century romantics residing in Venice.

Byron and Shelley rode along its sands and bathed in its waters, John and Effie Ruskin ambled along its shores, gathering shells and catching crabs, and Browning wrote fondly of afternoon walks on his 'beloved' Lido.

By the turn of the 20th century, bathing establishments were open and the Lido had become one of the most fashionable holiday resorts in Europe. The prominent neo-Byzantine Excelsior Hotel opened in 1908, and a few years later the equally grand Hotel des Bains, now luxury apartments, provided the setting for Thomas Mann's novel *Death in Venice*.

The Lido today

The Lido no longer enjoys the exclusivity of the resort depicted in *Death in Venice*, but it is popular for its sea and sands, cinema and casino, and all the sporting activities that Venice itself cannot offer. It is at its most fashionable during the International Film Festival (*see p17*).

If you have become accustomed to the traffic-free streets of Venice it can be disconcerting to step out of the *vaporetto* and encounter cars, buses and taxis. The island's main attraction is its long stretch of fine sands.

It is worth a trip to the Lido just for the beauty of the return journey on a late summer evening. Little has changed since Shelley described the view of San Marco on approach from the Lido,

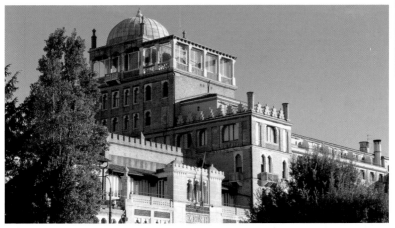

The Lido's Excelsior Hotel was frequented by fashionable society in the early 20th century

likening the temples and palaces to 'fabrics of enchantment piled to heaven'.

Beaches

The Lido's beach season lasts from mid-June to mid-September. In a recent survey, it was classified among the hundred cleanest beaches in Italy. However, the proximity of the heavily industrialised towns of Mestre and Marghera may put you off the idea of a dip. The only public beaches lie to the northern and southern ends of the island. Between them lie the finely manicured sands of those beaches which are controlled by hotels. (For watersports and other activities on the Lido, *see pp162–3.*)

Old Jewish cemetery

The first Jewish cemetery in Venice, it was founded in 1386 in the grounds of the monastery of San Nicolò. Regularly maintained, it is worth visiting to see

the surviving tombstones of eminent Italian Jews.

Via Cipro, San Nicolò. Guided tours, tel: 04 171 5359. Admission charge.

The Lido has a good boat service from Venice. Vaporetti routes: Nos 1, 8, LN, 51/52 & 61/62. Also 2 in summer. The journey from Riva degli Schiavoni takes 12–20 minutes, No LN being the quickest boat. The arrival point on the Lido is Piazzale Santa Maria Elisabetta, from where you can take a bus or taxi, hire a bike or walk.

Murano

Occasionally described as a mini-Venice, the island of Murano is made up of small islands divided by canals and linked by bridges. It cannot really be compared to the historic city, though it does have its own Grand Canal, a few surviving old palaces and a handsome Veneto-Byzantine basilica.

In the 16th century the island was a pleasure ground for noble Venetians, full of villas, gardens and fountains. The population grew to 30,000; now it's down to a mere 8,000. However, Murano has not changed in all respects, glass still being its *raison d'être*.

Museo del Vetro (Museum of Glass)

Housed in Palazzo Giustinian, this splendid collection of antique glass traces the story of glass production from Roman times to the 18th century. The majority of exhibits date from Murano's glass-making heyday. The most celebrated piece is the 15th-century **Coppa Barovier** (*see p139*).
Palazzo Giustinian, Fondamenta Giustinian 8, Isola di Murano. Tel: 04 173 9586. www.museiciviciveneziani.it. Open: Apr–Oct daily 10am–6pm; Nov–Mar daily 10am–5pm. Admission charge.

Santi Maria e Donato

The splendid Veneto-Byzantine basilica stands on the former main square of Murano. Founded in the 7th century, it was rebuilt in its present form in the 12th century and dedicated to the Virgin Mary. San Donato was a 4th-century bishop whose body was brought here in 1125 from Cephalonia. With his relics came the bones of a dragon he is said to have slain with spit. The dragon's 'remnants' can still be seen behind the Baroque altar.

The oldest feature of the church is the splendid colonnaded apse on the canal, with its double tier of arches,

dog-tooth moulding and marble zigzag patterns. Though heavily restored, the interior retains the form of a basilica and is striking in its impact. The eye is drawn to the Byzantine mosaic above the apse, depicting a Madonna standing in prayer against a gold background.

The greatest treasure of the church is the 12th-century mosaic *pavimento*, decorated with ornamental motifs and animals.
Campo San Donato. Tel: 04 173 9056. Open: Mon–Sat 9am–noon & 3.30–7pm, Sun 3.30–7pm (6pm in winter).

San Pietro Martire

Those who are saturated by glass souvenirs should feast their eyes on Giovanni Bellini's glorious *Madonna and Saints* in the Church of San Pietro Martire. This richly coloured altarpiece, fully restored, shows St Augustine and St Mark presenting the kneeling Doge Agostino Barbarigo to the Virgin.

San Pietro Martire is a Gothic church rebuilt in the 15th century. The massive, early 20th-century chandeliers were, of course, made by Muranese glassworkers.
Fondamenta dei Vetrai. Tel: 04 173 9704. Open: daily 9am–noon & 3–6pm. Closed: Sun morning.

Murano is reached by Vaporetti Nos LN, 13 & 41/42 from Fondamente Nuove.

Burano

Lined with lace stalls and brightly coloured houses, Burano is a small

Murano's Santi Maria e Donato

island of nearly 5,000 people, some 8km (5 miles) from Venice in the northern lagoon.

Casa Bepi

To see the most colourful house in the lagoon, take the tiny alley opposite the Galuppi restaurant in the Via Baldassare Galuppi. This brings you to a small square where you can't miss the multicoloured geometrical façade of Casa Bepi at No 339.

Museo del Merletto (Lace Museum)

This is one of the few places in Burano where it is a guarantee that you will see authentic Burano lace. Visitors can watch the local women busily stitching in the old tradition.

Piazza Baldassare Galuppi. Tel: 04 173 0034. www.museiciviciveneziani.it. At time of going to press, the museum was closed for restoration and due to

reopen in spring 2011. Check website or call for opening times. Admission charge.

Via Baldassare Galuppi

Burano's main street, which is lined with lace and linen shops and fish restaurants, is named after a local 18th-century operatic composer. Piazza Baldassare Galuppi's most distinctive feature is the precariously tilting *campanile* of the Church of San Martino.

No LN for Burano (change for Torcello) leaves Fondamente Nuove in Venice roughly every half hour. The journey takes 40–50 minutes. LN from San Zaccaria via the Lido and Punta Sabbioni takes about 1½ hours.

Torcello

At first sight Torcello appears to be no more than a marshy, abandoned islet, and (Cont. on p134)

Life in the lagoon

To describe the Venetian lagoon as 'A Piece of Eden' – the title of a guidebook on the lagoon – is perhaps an overstatement. It is certainly beautiful in a bleak, melancholic way, particularly in the early hours of the evening, but the low-lying islands, some semi-submerged in the seawater, are essentially made up of salt marshland and mudbanks. The occasional vine or vegetable garden flourishes, but most of the woodland disappeared long ago.

Islands that were once densely populated are now deserted and overgrown. Many of them have a tale to tell: San Clemente, for instance, was once famous for literary gatherings and feasts attended by the doge; Madonna del Monte was a powder magazine for the Republic; and San Servolo was a Benedictine monastery, then a lunatic asylum, and is now the site of Venice International University (*www.univiu.org*).

The crested pochard drake has returned to the lagoon after increased conservation efforts

The great egret now frequents the protected lagoon

For centuries the islands and waters of the lagoon have been popular hunting territory. Records show that the first doge trapped birds here and hunted game. In the 18th century the aristocracy spent long hours on the lagoon, going out in gondolas or light boats, equipped with nets, snares, crossbows, blowpipes, dogs, hawks or whatever the latest trend dictated. The wild boar and deer that frequented the then ubiquitous forestland disappeared in the 19th century. Nowadays, the only targets for hunters are ducks.

Today, you have to look hard for the wildlife. Massive industry at Marghera, the lack of a proper sewage system and a profusion of algae have not produced the ideal environment. However, thanks to a campaign to protect and conserve the lagoon, it is at least cleaner than it was 20 years ago. Species that have happily survived are the egrets, which strut in the sandy shallows, the Adriatic lizards, whose bright green spring coats can be spotted among the sand dunes, and a large variety of ducks. The waters provide the city with plenty of shellfish, and there are now over two dozen fish farms set up in the wide-open areas closed off from the sea, not to mention protected nesting areas on the Lido.

it is hard to believe that this was once the centre of a flourishing civilisation. The first inhabitants may have come here as early as the 5th century, fleeing from the barbarians on the mainland.

Over the centuries, churches and palaces were constructed, and the population rose to an estimated 20,000. The decline started when the waterways silted up, leading to a fall-off in trade and a malaria epidemic. The inhabitants deserted the island for the more inviting settlement of the Rivus Altus, the group of islands in Venice which later became known as the Rialto.

Today, all that remains on Torcello are a handful of houses and the splendid cathedral and church, lying, as John Ruskin put it, 'like a little company of ships becalmed on a faraway sea'.

Attila's Seat

Tradition has it that this ancient stone chair in the *piazza* was used by the king of the Huns. More probably, it served as the judge's seat in local tribunals.

Cattedrale di Santa Maria dell'Assunta

Generally regarded as the oldest building in the whole lagoon, it is certainly one of the most exceptional. Founded in 639 to house the relics of Torcello's first bishop, the cathedral was rebuilt in similar style from the 9th to the 11th centuries.

The crypt and the foundations of the baptistery in front of the main portal date from the original church. The interior is simple and dignified and,

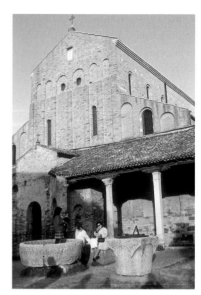

Torcello's Byzantine cathedral

despite restoration over the centuries, looks very similar to how the church must have appeared 900 years ago. It is decorated with beautiful Byzantine mosaics, the most compelling of which is the 13th-century *Madonna and Child*, set against a glowing gold background in the central apse, with a frieze of Apostles below. Offsetting this, a turbulent mosaic of *The Last Judgement and Apotheosis of Christ* occupies the entire western wall. Dividing the church, the iconostasis is made of marble panels carved with peacocks, lions and foliage, surmounted by a frieze of 15th-century paintings of the Virgin and Apostles.
Tel: 041 296 0630. Open: Apr–Oct daily 10.30am–6pm; Nov–Mar daily 10am–5pm. Admission charge.

Church of Santa Fosca

Santa Fosca is an elegant little church, built in the late 11th century to house the relics of Santa Fosca. On five sides it is surrounded by a portico, which links it to the cathedral. Inspired by the inventions of the East, the church has marble pillars and a stunning mosaic pavement. Architecturally it is one of the finest buildings in the entire lagoon.

Museo dell'Estuario (Museum of the Lagoon)

Two of Torcello's surviving *palazzi* house local archaeological finds from the 6th to the 12th centuries and a mixed collection of mosaics, paintings, icons and jewellery.
Palazzo del Consiglio. Tel: 04 173 0761. Open: Apr–Oct Tue–Sun 10.30am– 5.30pm; Nov–Mar Tue–Sun 10am–5pm. Closed public holidays. Admission charge.

THE TRADITION OF LACE

In the 16th century Venetian lace, and particularly 'Burano point', was in great demand in Europe. Foreign courts tried to steal the craft by luring Venetian lacemakers abroad. The industry slumped with the fall of the Republic but a revival took place in 1872, when a lacemaking school was established on Burano. Once again the lace and embroidery enriched the trousseaux of the aristocracy of Europe.

Today, the majority of lace and embroidery that you see draped over street stalls comes from the Far East, which accounts for the cheap prices. An authentic handmade Burano tablecloth takes months of painstaking work and bears a correspondingly high price tag.

Torcello is reached by Ferry No T from neighbouring Burano. The journey takes 5 minutes.

THE MAINLAND

Given the splendour of Venice, and the fact that the Veneto was formerly little more than an offshoot of the great Venetian empire, it is perhaps not surprising that its provincial cities are largely ignored by tourists. Those who do discover the region will find it refreshingly free of tourists – with the notable exception of Verona.

Watered by rivers and canals, the Veneto is a large, lush plain enclosed within the contrasting boundaries of the Dolomiti (Dolomites) to the north, the shores of Lake Garda to the far west, the delta of the Po to the south and the Venetian lagoon to the east.

The historical link with Venice has left its mark. Medieval town centres, either preserved or restored, are strong on art and architecture, while the countryside and the banks of the Brenta are graced by Andrea Palladio's perfectly proportioned classical villas.

A further appeal of the region is the cuisine, which is usually superior to, and always cheaper than, that of Venice. There is also a handful of particularly attractive country villa hotels. The following suggested excursions are only a few of the highlights of the Veneto. Each can be covered in a day from Venice, with the exception of Verona, whose historic attractions merit an overnight stay. If you are travelling around by car, bear in mind that some of the historic centres are surrounded by modern sprawl and getting there may take longer than you think.

Asolo

The jewel of the Venetian hilltop towns, Asolo lies in the foothills of the Dolomites, surrounded by slopes of cypress trees and vines. At the end of the 15th century, the Venetian-born Caterina Cornaro, deposed queen of Cyprus, arrived in Asolo and established a Renaissance court here. One of her literary entourage, Cardinal Bembo, coined the word *asolare*, meaning 'to idle away time'.

Resplendent with greenery, Asolo offers a taste of rural Italy

Even in modern times it is not difficult to see how this little oasis, with its medieval dwellings, arcaded streets and gardens, induced a life of *il dolce far niente* (sweet idleness). For centuries the hill town has lured artists, writers and musicians. It was a favourite haunt of Robert Browning, who resided in what is now the luxury Hotel Villa Cipriani and entitled his last volume of poems *Asolando*.

Asolo is 65km (40 miles) northwest of Venice, reached by train to Treviso, then a bus to the outskirts of Asolo and connecting minibus to the centre.
Tourist office: Piazza Garibaldi 73. Tel: 042 352 9046. www.asolo.it

Bassano del Grappa

Famous for grappa and majolica pottery, the town of Bassano is set at the mouth of the River Brenta. Despite devastation during both World Wars and the spread of modern industry, it manages to preserve its historic centre of ancient buildings and arcaded streets. The paintings of the local Da Ponte family, who were all called Bassano, can be seen in the Civic Museum.

76km (47 miles) northwest of Venice, reached by train from Venice.
Tourist office: Largo Corona d'Italia 35. Tel: 042 452 4351.

By boat along the Brenta

From the 16th century to the fall of the Republic, many Venetian nobles took a boat called the *Burchiello* to their pleasure villas along the Brenta Canal.

Today, you can follow their itinerary, also on a boat called the *Burchiello*. While this modern white motorboat, seating 200 and equipped with armchairs and a bar, is hardly a replica of the original, it makes a very pleasant, if costly, way of travelling to Padua. The canal is 36km (22 miles) long and the guided tour lasts 8½ hours.

The boat leaves from San Marco and crosses the lagoon to enter the Brenta at Fusina. With luck, you might stop to see the interior of Palladio's well-known Villa Foscari, which today stands uncomfortably close to Mestre's oil refineries. Also known as La

Malcontenta, the villa is decorated with 16th-century frescoes.

On the way upstream you will pass more than 70 villas, many of them set in fine gardens. The other villas normally visited by the boat are the Barchessa Valmarana at Mira Porte, built in the early 18th century and transformed not long after in French Baroque style, and the grand Villa Pisani at Stra, adorned
(*Cont. on p140*)

The mainland

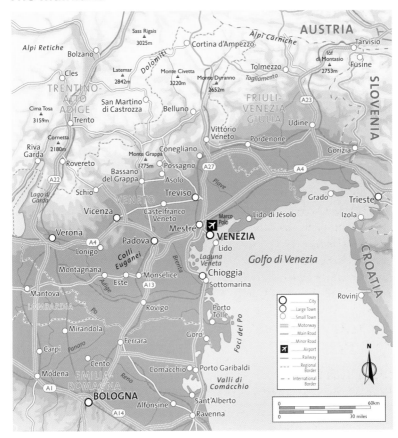

A galaxy of glass

Glass has been made in Venice for more than a thousand years. The furnaces were originally established in the historic centre, but because of the fire risks they were moved to the island of Murano in 1291. Here it was hoped that the secrets of the Venetian craft would be closely guarded.

A glassmaker was granted privileges that were unparalleled among other artisans, but if he left the island, he did so on penalty of death. The deterrent did not stop a few craftsmen absconding abroad, lured by the tempting rewards offered by foreign kings and nobles.

A visit to a Murano glass-blowing factory is a must

Over the centuries, the Venetians have created an impressive range of glass. Some of the most original pieces are the richly coloured enamelled cups and glasses decorated with erotic scenes or portraits of couples. The prize piece in Venice is the blue Barovier Nuptial Cup (1470–80), decorated by Angelo Barovier, one of the members of the famous Barovier dynasty of Muranese glassmakers.

The 16th century saw high demand for the production of the most beautiful of all the Venetian-blown glass – the clear, colourless *cristallo*, which was reproduced in paintings by Titian and Veronese.

This was followed by the invention and mastery of endless new techniques designed to achieve different effects. These included glass gilded with leaf, fired and frosted glass, filigree glass, and opaque white glass, which was popularly twisted into cables or threads.

The fall of the Republic inevitably led to the decline of the glassworks, but the tradition was revived again in the 1850s. Today, the glass factories of Murano and the ubiquitous glass shops here and in Venice are eloquent evidence that the industry, though not what it was in the 16th century, is still going strong. Shops and showrooms have dazzling displays of glass, from kitsch souvenirs to chandeliers fit for

Venetian glass is famous the world over

kings. Don't assume, however, that all that glitters is glass from Murano. Much of it is cheap imitation from the East.

No visit to Murano is complete without a visit to a glass factory (see 'Shopping', *p153*) – not necessarily to see the showrooms (the typically bright colours and ornate design are not to everyone's taste) but to watch a glass-blowing maestro miraculously transform a blob of molten glass paste into the perfect shape of a vase, bird or mammal.

with frescoes by Giambattista and Giandomenico Tiepolo.

From here, a bus takes you to Padova (Padua) for your return trip to Venice by coach to Piazzale Roma – which is something of an anticlimax after the outward trip by boat. The more economical alternative to the *Burchiello* is to follow the canalside road by car or take the Venice–Padua bus to Stra.

The Burchiello *service runs from late Mar to early Nov. The Venice to Padua direction operates on Tue, Thur & Sat; Padua to Venice on Wed, Fri & Sun. Reservations (essential) can be made through travel agents and hotels in Venice, or through www.ilburchiello.it*

The towers of Bassano del Grappa (see p136)

Castelfranco Veneto

This small, walled town's main claim to fame is as the birthplace of painter Giorgione. His house has been turned into a museum. The Castelfranco *Madonna in the Duomo* is one of the very few paintings which is universally accepted as a Giorgione.

45km (28 miles) northwest of Venice, reached by train. Tourist office: Via F.M. Preti 66. Tel: 043 249 5000. www.prolococastelfrancoveneto.it

Chioggia

Lying at the southern end of the Venetian lagoon, 25km (15½ miles) from Venice, Chioggia is one of the most important seafaring and fishing centres of the Adriatic.

With its canals and narrow streets, it is often compared to Venice – or at least to the more humble quarters of the historic city. However, the notable presence of cars and the straightness of its streets and canals make it feel very different. In fact, several of its canals have been filled in to provide additional roads for cars.

Historically, the port is best known for the great war of Chioggia in 1380, when the Venetians finally defeated their naval rivals, the Genoese. Losses on both sides were high and, sadly, a great deal of medieval Chioggia was reduced to ruins.

Like Venice, Chioggia is connected to the mainland by a modern causeway. The journey by land and water makes a pleasant excursion from Venice, particularly if you arrive in the morning to see Chioggia's famous fish market.

Corso del Popolo

The main thoroughfare, lined with shops and restaurants, splits the island into two. At the southern end, the 14th-century *duomo* (cathedral) in Piazza Vescovile was largely destroyed by fire and rebuilt by Baldassare Longhena in 1624. There is a painting attributed to Tiepolo in the chapel to the left of the altar, among other 18th-century works of art.

One of the street's oldest buildings, heavily restored, is the early 14th-century Granary with the external relief *Madonna* by Sansovino. The fish market lies behind it. The Corso del Popolo ends at Piazzetta Vigo by the port. Cross the Ponte Vigo over the Canale della Vena to reach the Church of San Domenico, which contains Carpaccio's painting of *St Paul* (1520), his last known work.

Sottomarina

Once a fishing village, this is now Chioggia's unremarkable seaside resort.

Chioggia is 25km (15½ miles) south of Venice. The quickest route is by bus from Piazzale Roma (50 minutes). Far more scenic is the route by bus and boat: bus No 11 from the Lido (roughly every hour) to Alberoni, then a ferry, then bus again to Pellestrina, and motonave (motorboat) to Chioggia. The whole journey takes about 90 minutes.

Colli Euganei (Euganean Hills)

The hot muds and the fine wines of the Euganean Hills have been drawing spa

enthusiasts and oenophiles since Roman times. The prettiest of the villages is **Arquà Petrarca**, where the Roman poet Petrarch spent his last years. His villa, Casa del Petrarca, is open to the public.

On the fringes of the Euganean Hills, the old walled towns of Montagnana, Este and Monsélice all merit a visit. *The Colli Euganei are easily accessible from Padua by bus or car, or from Venice by train (Montegrotto, Terme Euganee or Abano stations).*

Conegliano

Birthplace of the artist Cima da Conegliano (1460–1518), the town is equally famous as the centre of Prosecco production, the delightful sparkling white wine which flows throughout the Veneto. Wine buffs can follow well-established white- and red-wine routes, tasting at *trattorie* along the way. The town is largely industrial, with an old town on the hill above. *60km (37 miles) north of Venice, reached by train.*
Tourist office: Via XX Settembre 61. Tel: 04 382 1230.

Padova (Padua)

An ancient university town, Padua has a long-standing scholarly and cultural tradition. The university was founded in 1222, making it one of the oldest in Europe. In addition to its lure as a seat of learning, Padua brings in flocks of pilgrims, who come to worship the relics of St Anthony, and a stream of visitors to see Giotto's frescoes in the Cappella degli Scrovegni. The old part of the city is characterised by cobbled arcaded streets, bookshops and student cafés.

Padua is 37km (23 miles) west of Venice, linked by a regular train service. Tourist office: Piazzale della Stazione (railway station). Tel: 049 875 2077. www.turismopadova.it

Cappella degli Scrovegni

No visit to Padua is complete without a visit to Giotto's frescoes. His cycle of paintings, marking the break with Byzantine art, is one of the most important works in Italian painting. Depicting scenes from the New Testament, the cycle was created when Giotto (*c.*1266–1337) was at the height of his power: you do not have to be an art connoisseur to appreciate the dramatic intensity and the passion in these works of art.

Familiar outline of a domed basilica in Padua

Tel: 049 201 0020. www.cappella degliscrovegni.it. Open: daily 9am–7pm (occasionally until 10pm). Advance booking compulsory, as visitor numbers are limited. Admission charge.

Il Santo (Basilica di Sant'Antonio)

The richly decorated Romanesque-Gothic church, with its seven domes, minaret-style spires and two *campaniles*, looks distinctly oriental. Built between 1232 and 1307 to house the relics of St Anthony of Padua, the church is an important pilgrimage centre, particularly on 13 June, when the saint's death is commemorated.

One of the great pieces of Italian Renaissance sculpture, the *Gattamelata* equestrian monument by Donatello, stands in front of the basilica.

Tel: 049 822 5652 (Information Office). www.basilicadelsanto.it. Open: Apr–Oct Mon–Fri 6.20am–7.45pm, Sat–Sun 6.20am–7.45pm; Nov–Mar Mon–Fri 6.20am–7pm, Sat–Sun 6.20am–7.45pm. Free admission.

Treviso

Apart from the famous red chicory it produces and the fact that it is home to Luciano Benetton, Treviso has an attractive old centre of cobbled streets, waterways and porticoed houses. Much of it has been restored or rebuilt since the devastation of World War II, including medieval frescoes on town houses. The main sights are the cathedral and the churches of Santa Caterina and San Nicolò.

Verona's Roman arena

30km (18¹/₂ miles) northwest of Venice, reached by train. Tourist office: Piazza Monte di Pietà 8. Tel: 042 254 7632.

Verona

The great tourist magnet of the Veneto is the lovely city of Verona. The characters from Shakespeare's *Romeo and Juliet* probably never existed, but the balcony from where Juliet listened to her beloved, and the tomb where she is supposedly buried, fire the imagination of visitors from all over the world.

Verona is a city of remarkable classical ruins, medieval churches, museums, *piazzas* and galleries.
Verona is 114km (71 miles) west of Venice, reached by train. Tourist office: Via Degli Alpini 9. Tel: 045 806 8680. www.tourism.verona.it

Arche Scaligeri

In front of the small Romanesque church of Santa Maria Antica are the grand, finely sculpted Gothic tombs of

the Della Scala dynasty, the powerful and ruthless rulers of Verona from 1260 to 1387.
Via delle Arche Scaligeri, Piazza dei Signori.

Arena

This is one of the best-preserved and largest Roman amphitheatres in existence. An earthquake in the 12th century damaged huge chunks of the outer wall, but the interior was left more or less unscathed. The arena makes a magnificent setting for opera and ballet, with performances in July and August, and is also a great venue for rock and pop concerts.
Piazza Brà. Tel: 045 800 5151 (call centre). www.arena.it. Open: Jul & Aug daily 8.30am–7.30pm (mid-afternoon closure on performance days). Admission charge.

Basilica of San Zeno Maggiore

One of the finest Italian Romanesque churches, the Basilica of San Zeno

Maggiore has superb relief carvings on its portal and bronze doors.

The fine Gothic ceiling inside has 14th-century frescoes and the greatest art treasure of the city, Mantegna's triptych of the *Madonna and Child with Saints*.
Piazza San Zeno. Tel: 04 559 2813. www.chieseverona.it. Open: Mar–Oct Mon–Sat 8.30am–6pm, Sun 1–6pm; Nov–Feb Tue–Sat 10am–1pm & 1.30–5pm, Sun 1–5pm. Admission charge.

Castelvecchio

The former stronghold of the Scala family is now the Civic Museum of Art, where paintings, sculpture, and modern architecture by Carlo Scarpa, are complemented by fine views.
Corso Castelvecchio 2. Tel: 045 806 2611. www.comune.verona.it/ castelvecchio/cvsito. Open: Mon 1.30–7.30pm, Tue–Sun 8.30am–7.30pm. Admission charge.

Venetian villas

The Veneto is rich in Palladian villas built during the 1540s and 1550s for the wealthy merchants of Venice and Vicenza. The majority are now privately owned but there are some you can visit on certain days of the week.

Palladian's basic formula for the perfect villa was a central, symmetrical block, with an exterior portico and long wings of farm buildings where the labourers lived. He played on this basic theme, varying his style from stark simplicity to sprightly elaboration. The villas designed along the banks of the

Palladio's well-known Villa Foscari

Brenta became the prototype for idyllic 18th-century country estates in England and the USA.

La Rotonda

Considered to be Palladio's *pièce de résistance*, this is a masterpiece of symmetry which was the inspiration for Chiswick House in London and Thomas Jefferson's Monticello in the USA.
Vicenza. Tel: 044 432 1793. www.villa larotonda.it. Villa open: mid-Mar–early Nov Wed & Sat 10am–noon & 3–6pm. Grounds open: all year Tue–Sun 10am–noon & 3–6pm. Admission charge.

Villa Barbaro

Also known as Villa di Maser, this unique combination of Palladian architecture and Veronese frescoes makes this one of the finest Palladian villas.
7km (4 miles) east of Asolo, at Maser. Tel: 042 392 3004. www.villadimaser.it. Open: Mar–Oct Tue, Sat, Sun & public holidays 3–6pm; Nov–Feb weekends & public holidays 2.30–5pm, though opening times can vary from month to month. Admission charge.

Villa Foscari ('La Malcontenta')

See p137.
Tel: 041 547 0012. www.lamalcontenta. com. Open: Apr–Oct Tue & Sat 9am–noon. Other visits by appointment. Admission charge. Reached by bus to Malcontenta from Piazzale Roma or by boat along the Brenta Canal.

Vicenza's Basilica Palladiana

Villa Valmarana

Also called 'dei Nani', this villa is embellished with frescoes by Giambattista Tiepolo and his son, Giandomenico.
Via dei Nani 2, Vicenza. Tel: 044 432 1803. www.villavalmarana.com. Open: mid-Mar–early Nov Tue–Sun 10am–noon & 3–6pm; early Nov–mid-Mar Sat & Sun 10am–noon & 2–4.30pm. Admission charge.

Vicenza

Known as 'The City of Palladio', Vicenza certainly bears the mark of the renowned 16th-century architect. The Basilica, the palaces lining the main street, and the Teatro Olimpico are all works designed by him. Of these, the Teatro, a complex reconstruction of a Roman theatre, is the masterpiece. Classical plays are performed here in September.
Vicenza is 51km (32 miles) west of Venice, reached by train. Tourist office: Piazza dei Signori 8. Tel: 04 445 441. www.vicenzae.org

Getting away from it all

She was never loved. She was always the outsider, always envied, always suspected, always feared.
She fitted into no convenient category of nations.
She was the lion who walked by herself.

Jan Morris, *Venice*, 1960

Gardens

Venice is well known for its sparsity of green, open spaces, and more trees and benches have now been provided by the local council for footsore travellers.

Giardini ex Papadopoli

Unremarkable as gardens, these at least make a pleasant and shady alternative to Piazzale Roma if you happen to be waiting for a bus.
East of Piazzale Roma. Landing stage: Piazzale Roma.

Giardini Pubblici (Public Gardens)

These only real public gardens of the city were created by Napoleon: six ecclesiastical buildings were knocked down in the process. The greenery and open spaces provide welcome respite from the city centre, and the tall trees offer plenty of shade in the hot summer months. There are a few unnamed and knocked-about statues half hidden in the bushes, a disused bandstand, and a small playground. Beyond the Giardini Pubblici, the **Parco delle Rimembranze** is a large park with pine trees and red benches where you can sit and admire the sweeping panorama across the lagoon.
Landing stage: Giardini or Giardini Biennale.

Giardini ex Reali (Royal Gardens)

The great advantage of this small public garden is the benches within spitting distance of Piazza San Marco – and toilet facilities. Trees provide some shade but, being so central, the park is by no means peaceful.
South of Piazza San Marco, set back from the waterfront.

Parco Savorgnan

Frequented by local children for the playground, this park boasts unusually old, shady trees. Lying just off the Canale de Cannaregio, it is signposted from Campo San Geremia.
Landing stage: Ponte delle Guglie.

Minor islands of the lagoon
Forte di Sant'Andrea
Designed by the great military engineer
Michele Sanmicheli, this mighty Istrian
stone fortification was built between
1535 and 1549 on the island of Le
Vignole to guard the main entrance of
the lagoon. The fort was badly eroded
by the sea, but has been restored. It was
in the channel here that the doge
annually cast a gold ring into the water,
symbolising the marriage of Venice
with the sea.
Isola di Sant'Andrea.

San Francesco del Deserto
Of all the islands in the lagoon
accessible to the public, this is the
prettiest and most peaceful. Among the
dark mass of cypresses there is no more
than a small church, a 14th-century
cloister, a profusion of plants and a
handful of Franciscan friars.

There is a story attached to it: St
Francis of Assisi, on his way back from
Soria in 1220, took refuge on the island
during a raging storm and built a
chapel here. Later, the island was given
to the Franciscans and a monastery was
established here.

There is no public waterbus to the
island. The only way of getting there is
by an exorbitantly priced water-taxi,
from the island of Burano. The cost will
include the return journey and waiting
time at the island.

One of the friars will show you
round the monastery and gardens.
The church is unremarkable but

The tranquil monastery on the island of San
Francesco del Deserto

the cloister and gardens are quite
delightful.
*Convento di San Francesco del Deserto.
Tel: 041 528 6863. www.isola-
sanfrancescodeldeserto.it. Open: Tue–Sun
9–11am & 3–5pm. No admission charge,
but donations welcome.*

San Lazzaro degli Armeni
This little island close to the Lido is one
of the most interesting in the lagoon.

A leper colony for four centuries and
named after the lepers' patron saint, the
island was given to the Armenians in
1717. The community, in Venice since
the 13th century, established an
oratory in 1496 near Piazza San Marco,
which then became the Church of
Santa Croce.

Monastic cloisters on the island of San Lazzaro degli Armeni

The **monastery** on San Lazzaro degli Armeni was founded by an Armenian monk called Mechitar ('The Comforter') in 1717, and the island became a thriving centre of Armenian culture. Under Napoleon, it was the only monastery to escape suppression and to carry on its own cultural life. The community still continues its scholarly pursuits: if you visit the island, one of the monks will give you a guided tour. This covers the church, the cloister, the library with more than 35,000 precious volumes, the printing press established in 1789 and printing in 32 languages, and a museum housing pottery, archaeological finds and a mixed collection of paintings.

You can also see the room where Byron worked when he visited the island to learn Armenian and assist in researching an Armenian–English dictionary. Browning and Proust were others among the literati who visited the island.

Monastery tel: 041 526 0104. Open: daily 3.25–5.25pm guided visit. Admission charge. Vaporetto: No 20 from Riva degli Schiavoni to Isola San Lazzaro degli Armeni.

Sant'Erasmo
Originally a holiday resort for the Romans, Sant'Erasmo is today devoted to vegetable-growing and fish-farming. This is the island whose long, curving form you can see for most of the journey from Venice to Burano and Torcello. The farms, open spaces and sandy shores provide a quiet respite from the streets of the city, and there are also decent eateries, but it is scenically and culturally unexciting.
Vaporetto: No 13 from Fondamente Nuove.

San Servolo
A monastery was founded here by Benedictine monks in the 9th century, and soon afterwards the establishment was also run as a hospital. From the 18th century until 1978, it served as an asylum, but since 1980 the island has had the happier role as a European centre for training craftsmen, and now also hosts the Venice International University, collaborating with five foreign universities.
Guided visits (daily 9.30am–5pm) can be booked. Tel: 041 524 0119. www.sanservolo.provincia.venezia.it. Vaporetto: No 20 from San Zaccaria.

Isola di San Michele
Since the early 19th century, the island of San Michele has served as the **cemetery** of Venice. Several illustrious

visitors to Venice are buried here, including Stravinsky, Ezra Pound and Diaghilev (who introduced Russian ballet to Europe in 1909, and died in Venice 20 years later). These are some of the lucky ones, whose bodies rest in peace. The majority are dug up after 12 years and taken to an ossuary, to make room for the newcomers. It can be somewhat disconcerting if you happen to see bulldozers unearthing the bones of those who have served their time.

Annexed to the cemetery is Mario Coducci's elegant Renaissance **Church of San Michele**, built in 1469. Faced in white Istrian stone, it stands prominently on the waterfront, the wake of the *vaporetti* splashing on its rocky shore. On the left, as you go in, is the pretty little **Cappella Emiliana**, a hexagonal marble chapel with three altarpieces. Access to the cemetery is via the church's delightful floral Gothic cloister.

Within the cemetery, signs indicate the various sections (called *recinti*) and the graves of the famous. Serge Diaghilev and Igor Stravinsky (together with his wife) lie in the Greek and Russian Orthodox area, while Ezra Pound rests in the somewhat neglected Protestant section (*Evangelici*). Despite signs, it is not easy to find your way among the seemingly endless rows of graves, tombs, monuments and mausoleums.

The whole place is a riot of colour, for nearly every grave has at least one vase of real or imitation flowers. If you go there on Sunday mornings or 2 November (the day of the dead), the *vaporetti* from Venice will be full of Venetians armed with huge bunches of flowers to place on the graves of loved ones.

The island of San Michele is reached by Nos 41/42 & 52 vaporetti from Venice. Cemetery open: daily 7.30am–4pm (6pm in summer). Church open: daily 7am–12.30pm & 3–4pm.

Getting away from it all

Isola di San Michele, seen from the lagoon

Shopping

Venice may have lost its role as the great European trading metropolis, but it is still a busy shopping centre. Window-fronts provide a visual feast with their dazzling displays of jewellery, fabrics, glass and masks. Those willing to explore the streets beyond San Marco will discover that Venetian craftsmanship still survives. Bookbinders, carpenters, mask-makers and even mosaicists can be found in small workshops off the beaten track.

The island of Murano is still an important centre for the glass industry, and Burano makes lace and linen. Along with the authentic articles sold throughout Venice comes a vast quantity of kitsch and imitation goods, from myriad mock-Murano glass objects to the imitation Gucci bags sold by African hawkers in main squares and thoroughfares.

The absence of cars is one of the obvious pleasures of shopping in Venice. You can stroll at leisure anywhere in the city, and all the main shopping areas are within walking distance of San Marco.

Shopping streets and areas

Piazza San Marco has a concentration of exclusive shops, selling top-quality jewellery, linen, lace and glass, all at predictably high prices. For designer boutiques and specialists in leather, knitwear and silk, concentrate on the streets west of the Piazza: Calle Vallaresso, Frezzeria, Salizzada San Moisè and Calle Larga XXII Marzo. **The Merceria**, running from Piazza San Marco to the Rialto, also has a number of top-of-the-range clothes and shoe boutiques, including Dolce & Gabbana, Gucci and Pollini. The **Rialto** is the cheapest area for leather and silk accessories, angora and lambswool sweaters, and typically Venetian souvenirs, though Chinese-owned leather goods stores are beginning to crop up around the city. **Strada Nova**, a busy thoroughfare of Cannaregio, is another of the less expensive shopping areas, though it lacks the atmosphere of the Rialto. For a more intimate, boutique-style shopping experience, head to Dorsoduro (in particular the San Pantalon area), where you can find great clothes, costume jewellery and designer homeware.

For glass, you should make a trip to the island of **Murano** (*see pp129–30*). Here you can watch the glass-blowers, visit showrooms and feast your eyes on a multitude of window-fronts stacked with every conceivable item that can be reproduced in glass.

The island of **Burano** (*see pp130–31*), traditional centre of lacemaking, has a lace school where you can see the genuine article displayed and being made. Stalls lining the streets usually sell cheaper, manufactured versions, some of it made in the Far East.

Markets and food shops

The Rialto market in the morning is one of the most colourful sights in Venice. Crates of fresh fruit and vegetables, much of it from the island of **Sant'Erasmo** (*see p148*), arrive on barges, which offload on to the banks of the Grand Canal. In summer, expect to see fruit stalls piled high with strawberries, peaches, figs, cherries, lemons and watermelons. Vegetable stalls are equally colourful, with gleaming peppers, aubergines, tomatoes, zucchini (courgettes) and the famous red *radicchio* from Treviso in winter.

The Pescheria (fish market) has an extensive display of fresh fish and seafood, including sole, skate, sea bass, sardines, squid and live shrimps still twitching in their trays. The Rialto also has some enticing delicatessens (*alimentari*), where you can pick up delicious cheeses, wines and *prosciutto*.

Open-air markets on a much more modest scale are held in other parts of the city, such as in **Campo Santa Maria Formosa**, **Campo Santa Margherita**, **Via Garibaldi** and **Strada Nova** near Ponte della Guglie.

Practicalities

Shops generally open from Monday to Saturday 8.30/9am–1pm and 4/5–7/8pm. Most food shops close on Wednesday afternoons. Nowadays, many shops are open on Sundays, particularly souvenir outlets in summer, and many of the designer boutiques in San Marco. Credit cards are accepted in virtually all shops. The Rialto food market (where cash will be required) is open Monday to Saturday, 8am–1pm, as is the Pescheria, though it is also closed on Monday.

Cartier is just one of many exclusive names in the shopping streets of Venice

Books, prints and marbled paper

Look out for small shops under the name of *legatoria* (bookbinder), which sell hand-printed paper. The paper was originally used to bind books and leaflets – now it is used to cover a variety of gifts, such as address books, boxes, photo albums and notebooks.

Prints and maps of the city, both historical and modern, are good value.

Alberto Valese–Ebru
Specialist in marbled paper and fabrics.
Campiello Santo Stefano, San Marco 3471.
Tel: 041 523 8830.

BAC Art Studio
Prints, hand-painted wooden frames, posters of Venice and Carnival.
San Vio, Dorsoduro 862.
Tel: 041 241 2716.
www.bacart.com

Fantoni Libri Arte
Specialist in art books.
Salizzada San Luca, San Marco 4119 .
Tel: 041 522 0700.

Legatoria Piazzesi
Hand-printed papers with distinctive marble design. Antique

woodblocks are still used to make the paper by the traditional *carta varese* method. Decorative boxes, frames, sketch books and card games.
Campiello della Feltrina, San Marco 2511c, near the Church of Santa Maria del Giglio.
Tel: 041 522 1202.

Rivoaltus
Beautifully hand-crafted diaries and address books.
Ponte di Rialto, San Polo 11. Tel: 041 523 6195.

Porto Daniela
Inexpensive prints and posters.
Rio terà dei Nomboli, San Polo 2753.
Tel: 041 523 1368.

Venice Pavilion Bookshop
Unbeatable selection of books on Venice.
Giardinetti ex Reali, San Marco 2.
Tel: 041 522 5150.

Sansovino
Art books, guides and literature on Venice.
Bacino Orseolo, San Marco 84.
Tel: 041 522 2623.

Libreria Marco Polo
Great selection of travel guides and books in English.

Salizzada San Lio, Castello 5467.
Tel: 041 522 6343. www. libreriamarcopolo.com

Fashion

Coin
Part of a good-quality chain of department stores with everything from fashion and perfume to kitchenware. Many of the locals shop here.
Salizzada San Giovanni Crisostomo, Cannaregio 5787, close to the Rialto.
Tel: 041 520 3581.
www.coin.it

Mori & Bozzi
The loveliest shoe shop in town. The coolest styles in the softest leather.
Rio terà Maddalena, Cannaregio 2367.
Tel: 041 715 261.

Ottico Fabbricatore
Über-stylish store specialising in designer eyewear and clothes in silks and cashmere.
Calle dell'Ovo, San Marco 4773. Tel: 041 522 5263.
www.otticofabbricatore. com

3856
Popular haunt of students with money to

burn, with quirky clothing and gorgeous accessories.
Calle San Pantalon, Dorsoduro 3749.
Tel: 041 720 595.

Glass

Venetians, and notably the Muranese, have been making glass for centuries (*see pp138–9*). Items can be packed and freighted, or sent by courier.

Barovier e Toso
Centuries-old family firm producing a vast range of glass, including vases, glasses, plates and chandeliers.
Fondamenta Vetrai 28, Murano. Tel: 041 739 049.
www.barovier.com

Carlo Moretti – L'Isola
Magnificent modern glassware.
Campo San Moisè, San Marco 1468.
Tel: 041 523 1973.
www.carlomoretti.com

Pagnacco
The world of animals in glass miniatures, alongside orchestras.
Mercerie San Marco 231.

Guglielmo Sent
This is one of the old family businesses. Speciality: glass necklaces and clocks.
Fondamenta Vetrai 8a, Murano.
Tel: 041 527 4966.

Marina e Susanna Sent
Part of the Sent dynasty, these sisters conjure

up beautiful glass jewellery.
Campo San Vio, Dorsoduro 669.
Tel: 041 520 8136. www. marinaesusannasent.com

Venini
Innovative and distinctive: all pieces are signed and dated.
Piazzetta dei Leoncini, San Marco 314.
Tel: 041 522 4045.
www.venini.com

Lace, linen and fabrics

Venetia Studium
Exquisite lamps in fine silks and soft furnishings in sumptuous velvets.
Calle Larga San Marco, San Marco 2403.
Tel: 041 522 9281.
www.venetiastudium.com

Trois
Exotic hand-printed fabrics, including Fortuny-inspired designs.
Campo San Maurizio, San Marco 2666.
Tel: 041 522 2905.

Leather

Plenty of shops sell leather but prices tend to be higher than in Florence and Rome. The best bet for leather shoes is the Mercerie.

The vegetable market entices shoppers with its exotic fare

For reasonably priced wallets, handbags, belts and gloves, make for the Rialto.

Masks

Since the Carnevale was reinstated in the late 1970s, mask shops have proliferated throughout the streets and squares of Venice. During the 18th century the wearing of masks was widespread, permitted by the state from Boxing Day to Shrove Tuesday. Mask shops did a roaring trade, supplying not only Italians but the many Europeans who prized the Venetian art of mask-making. Nowadays the wearing of masks is mainly restricted to the Carnevale, which takes place over the ten days before Shrove Tuesday.

The choice of masks sold in the city ranges from cheap factory imitations from Taiwan to beautifully crafted creations as worn in the heyday of the Carnevale. The majority are made of papier mâché (often 'cracked' to give an antique effect), though there are also masks made from leather and porcelain.

The word 'mask', or *maschera*, comes from the Lombard *maska*, meaning a dead person or the soul of the dead. While most of the masks you see in Venice represent characters from plays, others are linked with the underworld, often symbolising rites which cleansed all evil and ensured the fertility of the soul. At the other end of the scale are masks of beaming sunshines, long-nosed Pinocchios, jugglers, cats, and figures of Hansel and Gretel.

Many of the masks represent characters from plays performed by bands of actors who travelled through Italy from the 16th to the 18th centuries, and then moved on to France. The most familiar of these *Commedia dell'Arte* characters are Harlequin, Columbine, Pierrot, Brighella, Pucinella and Pantalone. Easily recognisable is the Dottore, traditionally from the old university town of Bologna. A caricature of intellectual vanity, usually giving a

A richly dressed mannequin advertises masks for sale

long pompous speech, he is dressed in a black gown with wide-brimmed hat and small spectacles.

In the heyday of the Carnevale, the most common disguise was *La Bauta*, comprising a *tricorne* hat, a black cape, and a mask known as the *larva* (the soul of the dead). This was the only disguise allowed during certain periods outside the Carnevale.

The following are some of the most intriguing mask shops in Venice, for browsing, buying, or watching the mask-maker at his trade.

Balocoloc

Stylish collection of masks, hats (including *tricorni*) and capes. *Calle Lunga Santa Croce 2134. Tel: 041 524 0551. www.balocoloc.com*

Ca' Macana

Masks, crafts and costumes. Fascinating selection, with masks being made on the spot. *Calle delle Botteghe, Dorsoduro 3172, close to Ca' Rezzonico. Tel: 041 520 3229. www.camacana.com*

La Ricerca

Exquisitely crafted masks in leather are the work of the talented Di Marchi brothers, who specialise in highly original objects. *Ponte delle Ostreghe, San Marco 2431. Tel: 041 521 2606.*

Mondo Novo

Wonderful selection of fantasy masks, including some of the most outrageous creations in town. Also supplies theatrical costumes. *Campo Santa Margherita (Rio Tera Canal), Dorsoduro 3063. Tel: 041 528 7344.*

La Trottola di Barbara

Specialist in papier mâché and ceramic masks; also carnival costumes. *Barbaria delle Tole, Castello 6468/9. Tel: 041 520 0204.*

Daniele Nason

Greek vases, friezes and tiles come in papier mâché here, along with unusual masks. *Calle della Mandola, San Marco 3715. Tel: 041 522 8113. www.nasondaniele.com*

Flavia

An irresistible shop crammed with papier mâché masks, flowing wigs and sumptuous carnival costumes. *Campo San Lio, Castello 5630. Tel: 041 528 7429. www.veniceatelier.com*

Tragicomica

Some of the most eye-catching masks in town, both tragic and comic. Specialists in *Commedia dell'Arte* masks. Feel free to watch them being made. *Calle dei Nomboli, San Polo 2800. Tel: 041 721 102. www.tragicomica.it*

Souvenirs

On the gondola theme, there are straw hats, striped shirts, gondoliers' slippers (velvet with rope soles), miniature silver gondolas and plastic gondolas that light up. The ultimate Venetian gift would be a *forcola*, the elegant wooden bracket for an oar on a gondola.

Saverio Pastor

Specialist artisan in *forcole* and oars. *Fondamenta Soranzo della Fornace, Dorsoduro 341. Tel: 041 522 5699. www.forcole.com*

Entertainment

With just a couple of nightclubs, Venice is hardly the city to choose for nightlife. The few young Venetians left in Venice nip across to Mestre to find the action after dark. Most tourists are content with a drink or two, a stroll through the streets and an early night.

Unlike in many European cities, you can feel quite at ease walking in the city late at night. Watering holes range from tiny offbeat bars, where you can rub shoulders with the locals, to sophisticated hotel piano bars and the famous Harry's Bar, which is still the place to spot the stars and sip a Bellini – prosecco and peach juice or syrup.

On the cultural scene, Venice offers opera throughout the year in the enchanting Fenice and Malibran theatres, and a wide choice of other music in churches and other venues.

Plays are performed in various theatres throughout the city, but usually only in Italian.

What's on

The main sources for listings are the *Nuova Venezia* and the *Gazzettino*

Santa Croce, lit up by night

GAMBLING

Gambling has always been a Venetian passion, but it was during the 17th and 18th centuries that the city was really hooked. In an attempt to control the vice in 1638, the state opened the Ridotto, a public gaming establishment housed in the old Palazzo Dandolo in Calle del Ridotto. The gaming rooms were open to rich and poor alike, the only condition being that players arrived in a mask.

The Ridotto was the cause of so many bankruptcies of Venetian families that in 1774 the Senate voted to shut it down, thereby forfeiting one of its largest sources of income. The closure did not put paid to private gambling, however, which carried on throughout the city in palaces, wine shops and coffee houses.

Today, the gambling habit carries on at the Casino Municipale, which was opened in the 1930s.

newspapers and the free booklets *Leo Bussola* and *Un Ospite di Venezia.*

Notices of forthcoming events are displayed on palace walls, in city squares and on large banners hanging from bridges. Tickets are available from agencies, through your hotel or, if it is a concert in a church, from the entrance of the venue on the day of the performance.

Casino

The Casino Municipale is located in the magnificent Palazzo Vendramin Calergi on the Grand Canal (*Strada Nuova, Cannaregio 2040. Tel: 041 529 7111. www.casinovenezia.it*). The premises open at 11am for the slot machines, while the tables operate from 3.30pm–2.30am. Dress smartly and take your passport or ID card.

A special ACTV launch runs between Piazzale Roma and the casino at San Marcuola, or the regular waterbus No 1 will get you there.

Palazzo Vendramin Calergi makes a fine setting for the casino

Cinema

Film aficionados flock to the Lido in late August/early September for the International Film Festival. This is held at Palazzo del Cinema, Lungomare Marconi (*Tel: Venice Biennale 041 521 8711. www.labiennale.org*), on the Lido, and, in Venice, at the **Giorgione cinema** and the outdoor cinema in Campo San Polo, which is erected from July until the end of the festival. **The Giorgione**, near Campo Santi Apostoli, is Venice's ony permanent cinema (*Cinema Giorgione, Rio Terra dei Franceschi,* *Cannaregio 4612. Tel: 041 522 6298. www.comune.venezia.it/cinema*). The Casa del Cinema occasionally has seasons of films in English (*Salizzada San Stae, Santa Croce 1990. Tel: 041 524 1320. www.comune.venezia.it/cinema*).

Gondola

The most enjoyable evening pursuit in Venice is gliding down the canals in a gondola (*see pp40–41*). Gondoliers tout throughout the city; alternatively, you can call for a gondola (*see p186*). If you cannot afford the exorbitant fees, make do with a No 1 night *vaporetto* down the Grand Canal, which goes sufficiently slowly to give you a glimpse of all the palaces. The boats run all night – when the number changes to N.

Music and theatre

In the 17th and 18th centuries, Venetian opera, music and theatre flourished in the works of Monteverdi (1567–1643), who was choirmaster at San Marco, Vivaldi (1678–1741), who was music master at the Ospedale della Pietà, and Goldoni (1707–93), the famous Venetian playwright. The first-ever opera house open to the public was inaugurated in Venice in 1637, and by the 18th century there were 19 theatres in the city, staging both operas and plays. Although Venice no longer boasts big names in music and theatre, it provides a broad spectrum of classical music events, including opera, ballet, recitals and symphonies.

The Fenice Productions

The beautiful Fenice theatre on Campo San Fantin is the only surviving opera house from the 18th century. Built in 1792, it has staged several important premieres, including Verdi's *Rigoletto* in 1851 and *La Traviata* (whose first staging was a fiasco) in 1853. It was first damaged by fire when originally under construction, then again in 1836 when the interior was completely destroyed. A year later the theatre was rebuilt exactly as before, rising 'like a phoenix' (*fenice*).

In 1996, the glorious pink and gilt Rococo interior was gutted again, and many of the contents, including priceless scores and archives, were destroyed. The efforts of the fire brigade were thwarted by the lack of water in nearby canals, which had been recently dredged for cleaning. An investigation into the cause of the fire concluded that it was arson. Happily, the glorious premises were reopened in 2004, and guided visits are held daily.

Operatic performances are also held in the delightfully restored Malibran theatre near the Rialto.

Reservations can be made at the Vela offices at the railway station, Piazzale Roma, or the Fenice theatre.
Tel: 041 940 200 (box office) or book at www.teatrolafenice.it

Classical concerts are also held in the **Frari Church**, the **Church of Santo Stefano** and the **Pietà** (where Vivaldi recitals are regularly performed). Look out for posters announcing them.

Interpreti Veneziani

A top-notch young orchestra (with 15 years' experience) performs Vivaldi, Mozart and other favourites at the **Chiesa di San Vidal** near the Accademia Bridge, on a nightly basis.
Campo Santo Stefano, San Marco 2862/B. Tel: 041 277 0561.
www.interpretiveneziani.com

Teatro Goldoni

This 800-seat theatre puts on plays by Goldoni, as well as contemporary drama, but only in Italian.

Calle Goldoni, San Marco 4650b. Tel: 041 240 2011. www.teatrostabileveneto.it

Late-night music

On rare occasions, jazz concerts are held in Venice, and the Goldoni theatre is one of the most popular venues. The following late-night bars/restaurants offer jazz or other live music throughout the year:

Al Chioschetto

Lovely waterside setting for summer concerts with reggae and jazz.
Zattere, Dorsoduro 1406a.
Tel: (mobile) 338 117 4077.

Le Bistrot de Venise

Wine bar/restaurant with good live music, regular art shows and poetry readings.
Calle dei Fabbri, San Marco 4685.
Tel: 041 523 6651.

Martini Scala Club

Smart piano bar and restaurant located near the Fenice theatre.

Campo San Fantin, San Marco 1980. Tel: 041 522 4121. Open until 3.30am.

Paradiso Perduto

Congenial late-night restaurant and bar with a variety of live music and good food.
Fondamenta della Misericordia, Cannaregio 2540.
Tel: 041 720 581.

Venice Jazz Club

One of the few places in town to enjoy cocktails and live jazz.
Fondamenta dei Pugni, Dorsoduro 3102.
Tel: 041 523 2056.
www.venicejazzclub.com

Music cafés

Hard Rock Café

Tucked behind Piazza San Marco, this café is great if you're missing your burgers and iced tea.
Bacino Orseolo, San Marco 1192.
Tel: 041 522 9665.
www.hardrock.com

A concert in Santo Stefano, one of Venice's loveliest churches

Children

Like all Italians, Venetians are indulgent towards children, but the city offers very few facilities for their amusement. There are not many play areas, and very few activities or events for the younger age group. Given the declining population of Venice, caused primarily by young families moving to Mestre, it is perhaps not surprising that the city has made little effort to create diversions for children.

On the plus side, children love riding on the *vaporetti* and watching the water traffic on the Grand Canal. After all, it is not often you see the postman in a launch or an ambulance without wheels. Other pleasurable pursuits are indulging in some street art with coloured chalk or joining the locals playing football in the city squares.

In the hot summer months, at least one trip to the Lido with the children will be obligatory. The Adriatic has shallow, safe waters, and there are several kilometres of sand as well as a good choice of sporting activities.

Carnevale and other festivals

Children love the Carnevale and many of them join in, dressing up in costumes and masks. The regattas and festivals (*see pp16–17*) will also provide plenty of colour and entertainment for the young. Starting at Christmas right through to the Carnevale, a funfair is held along Riva degli Schiavoni.

Glass-blowing

A glass-blowing demonstration is likely to fascinate any child. The island of Murano (*see pp129–30*) offers plenty of free demonstrations.

The Lido

Children's bikes, adult ones with child seats, tandems and four-wheeler family models can be hired on arrival. For a hefty fee, cabins can be hired on the beach. Lessons are available in sailing, windsurfing, waterskiing, canoeing, swimming and scuba diving. For information, contact the Excelsior Hotel beach office (*Tel: 041 526 0201*). Pedalos can also be hired on the beach.

Parks

Not accustomed to grass, most Venetian children play in the squares, either cycling, roller-skating or playing football. Watch out for the would-be Gattusos oblivious of passers-by.

The public gardens (*see p146*), which have a playground, provide the only green area of any size. More interesting than the gardens themselves is the incredible variety of boats that you can spot from the quayside skirting the park.

Rolling Venice

Children of 14 years or more are entitled to become members of Rolling Venice, an organisation set up to make the city more accessible to the younger generation (*see p187 for details*).

Sightseeing

Unless your children have a penchant for Venetian history and art, the only suitable museums are the Naval History Museum (*see p109*), particularly the models of Venetian ships, and the Natural History Museum (*see pp64–5*), which features some weird and wonderful creatures. The Peggy Guggenheim Collection at Palazzo Venier dei Leoni organises art workshops as part of their Kids' Day activities in English and Italian (*see pp84–5 for details*).

The Basilica can enthral a child, in small doses, with its dazzling mosaics and sense of mystery. The Doge's Palace is somewhat heavy-going for children, though the armoury, dungeons and tales of Casanova can all provide the young mind with diversions.

Parco Savorgnan has a great children's playground (*see p146*)

Sport and leisure

Lack of space precludes any proper sporting facilities in Venice itself. The Lido, however, has plenty to offer. The main season is from early June to mid-September, though non-watersports are usually available from early spring to late autumn. As with most things in Venice, prices are on the high side.

Flying and parachuting

For flying lessons or parachuting over Venice and the lagoon, contact the **Aeroclub G Ancillotto** on the Lido. *Aeroporto G. Nicelli, San Nicolò, Lido. Tel: 041 526 0808.*

Football

The local, second-division football club, Venezia, plays at home in the Pier Luigi Penzo stadium on Sant'Elena island. *Vaporetto Nos 1, 41/42, 51/52 & 61/62, or special football match boats. For tickets, contact HelloVenezia. Tel: 041 2424. www.hellovenezia.it*

Golf

The only course is the 18-hole **Circolo Golf Venice** (open to non-members). *Vila del Forte, Alberoni, Lido. Tel: 041 731 333. www.circologolfvenezia.it*

Motorboats

Visitors with a little experience can hire a boat from Cristiano Brussa (*Fondamenta di Cannaregio, Cannaregio 1030. Tel: 041 275 0196. www.cristiano brussa.com*). Otherwise houseboats are available for exploring the lagoon. *www.europeafloat.com/itvl.htm*

Riding

Riding and tuition are available at Circolo Ippico Venezia. *Via Cristoforo Colombo 41, Lido. Tel: 041 526 2028.*

Rowing and canoeing

Besides the Vogalonga marathon and the historical regatta (*see pp16–17*), more than 120 rowing races take place on the lagoon between April and October.

In all the events the boats are rowed 'Venetian-style'; that is, standing up and facing the direction in which you are going. For further information, contact the **Assessorato al Turismo del Comune di Venezia** (*Ca' Giustinian, San Marco 1364/A. Tel: 041 274 7735*).

For lessons and courses in rowing (and canoeing), apply to the **Circolo**

Canottieri Diadora (*Ca' Bianca, Lido. Tel: 041 526 5742*), or **Canottieri Bucintoro** (*Punta Dogana, Dorsoduro. Tel: 041 520 5630. www.bucintoro.org*).

municipal pool (*Tel: 041 715 650. www.ilcentrosantalvise.com*) – both are used mostly for lessons. Remember to take flip-flops and a swimming hat.

Sailing

Dinghies can be hired on the Lido beach in summer. Rental facilities and tuition are available from the **Excelsior Hotel**'s Sailing Club. Yachters can contact the marina on San Giorgio.

Scuba diving

Courses are offered by PADI instructors on the Lido. For more information, contact the **Excelsior Hotel** (*Tel: 041 526 0201*).

Swimming

Swimming in the Venetian lagoon is prohibited; not that you are likely to be tempted. There are several kilometres of sandy beach on the seaward side of the Lido. Large sections of the beach are organised by hotels which levy hefty charges for the use of facilities.

Alternatively, there are public beaches at Alberoni and Murazzi (accessible via Bus Line V) or San Nicolò (Bus Line B). Buses depart from Piazzale Santa Maria Elisabetta, close to the arrival point of the *vaporetti* from Venice.

The only hotels in historic Venice with a pool are the **Cipriani**, on the island of Giudecca, and the **Hilton Molino Stucky**. The **Rari Nantes** swimming pool (*Tel: 041 528 5430. www.rarinantesvenezia.it*) has restricted opening times, as does the **Sant'Alvise**

Tennis

There are plenty of opportunities for tennis on the Lido in summer. The following are the main clubs:
Tennis Club Ca' del Moro Lido
Via Ferruccio Parri 6. Tel: 041 770 965. www.tennisclubcadelmoro.it
Tennis Club Venezia
Lungomare Marconi 41/d. Tel: 041 526 0335. www.tennisclubvenezia.com

Waterskiing and windsurfing

Waterskiing and windsurfing are available on the Lido beach. See also the **Excelsior Hotel** (*Tel: 041 526 0201*).

Rowing is, unsurprisingly, a popular Venetian pastime

Food and drink

The Republic managed to produce some lavish feasts during its heyday, but Venice has never really been famed for its gastronomy. For years the staple diet has been polenta (maize), rice and fish. Although this is all local produce, it does not come cheap. Restaurant prices, particularly in the city centre, are around 30 per cent higher than on the mainland. Given these high costs and the variability of the cuisine, you may find that eating out is not the most rewarding of your Venetian experiences.

Gourmets, however, need not despair. There are restaurants serving first-rate Italian cuisine – some favourites are listed on *pages 167–9*. The less affluent will have to venture further afield to the small, off-the-beaten-track *trattorie* and cafés patronised primarily by Venetians. As a general rule you should avoid anywhere within spitting distance of Piazza San Marco.

In a city surrounded by a lagoon and so close to the sea, it is not surprising that fish predominates. A visit to the fish market at the Rialto will give you a good idea of what to expect on the menu.

Fish restaurants range from simple, family-run *trattorie* to smart establishments which lure you in with window displays of whole fresh fish, seafood and lobsters. On the menu of such establishments you can expect to see at least a few of the following: *San Pietro* (John Dory), *coda di rospo* (angler fish), *sogliola* (sole), *triglia* (red mullet), *cefalo* (grey mullet), *sarde* (sardines), *anguille* (eels), *gamberi*

(prawns), *calamari* (squid), *polpi* (octopus), *seppie* (cuttlefish) and *vongole* (clams). Fish is served in *antipasti*, in soups, in pasta, stuffed, fried or simply grilled or baked.

Pasta comes in all shapes and sizes. Sauces served most frequently are *alla marinara* (with mixed seafood) and *alle vongole* (with clams). *Bigoli*, a dark, wholemeal pasta, is served in *salsa*, with onion and anchovy sauce. Risottos, made with special rice, are excellent – either with seafood and shellfish or, occasionally, with meat and vegetables.

You'll be hard-pressed to find a vegetarian restaurant in Venice, but should have no difficulty in finding acceptable salads, pizzas, risottos and pastas on most menus. If you don't mind fish and seafood, you'll have no problem at all.

Given the stunning variety of fresh vegetables seen at stalls at the Rialto, you can find delicious, subtly flavoured asparagus, tender baby artichokes and colourful salad bowls of fennel, sorrel, peppers, celery, carrot and the famous *radicchio*, or red-leaved chicory, from Treviso.

With the exception of the most tourist-oriented *trattorie*, restaurants offer a choice of typically Italian fare, plus a few Venetian specialities. The following are those that you are most likely to come across on the local menus:

acciughe marinate: marinated anchovies with onions.

antipasto di mare: seafood hors-d'œuvres.

sarde in saor: a traditional Venetian dish of sardines marinated in a sauce of onions, spices, vinegar, pine kernels and sultanas; the strong sauce was at one time used to disguise the taste of poor-quality fish.

pasta e fagioli: a thick soup with pasta and beans – another local dish.

baccalà: dried cod, usually served as a creamy spread.

seppie in nero: cuttlefish cooked in its own ink.

risotto al nero di seppie: cuttlefish ink risotto.

risotto di mare: seafood risotto.

fegato alla veneziana: thin slivers of calves' liver served with a sauce of sautéed onion.

grigliata mista di pesce: mixed grilled fish.

Eating out

Eating places range from basic pizzerias to de-luxe restaurants. Many Venetians eat out regularly, whether it's merely a morning *cappuccino* and croissant from a bar, a sandwich or slice of pizza for lunch, or an evening out in a local restaurant.

Main meals are taken in a ristorante or *trattoria*: these days there is little

Venice may not be known for its gastronomy, but its restaurants and *trattorie* can't be beaten for their picturesque settings

difference between the two. The menu should clearly indicate the prices of dishes and the cost of the *coperto* (cover charge) and *servizio* (service).

In the summer months, if you see a restaurant full to overflowing, do not assume that the quality is high. Nor should you assume that elegant trappings mean elegant food. Décor is quite irrelevant to the standard of food.

Like all Italian cities, Venice has an abundance of pizzerias. These are cheaper than restaurants and are particularly popular with families. Many of them double up as *trattorie*, offering pasta dishes as well as pizzas.

Bars sell rolls or sandwiches. Locals tend to pay at the till and eat at the bar, which is much cheaper than sitting at a table with waiter service. But if there is a choice between standing by a hissing *cappuccino* machine and resting your feet alfresco with views of some beautiful square or canal, you may prefer to pay the extra.

For the price of a cup of coffee you can linger as long as you like.

WHERE TO EAT

The price range given in the listings refers to an average meal per person, excluding drinks:

£	less than €35
££	€35–50
£££	€50–70
££££	over €70

Wine with a meal costs from €5 a litre upwards. The cover charge varies from €1–4; service, at 12–15 per cent, may not be included in the bill. Restaurants are required to give you a receipt which by law you have to retain until you have left the establishment.

Restaurants normally close one day a week, and if they are serious about their fish this will be Monday, when the fish market is closed. Reservations are advisable at reputable restaurants and at peak times of the year.

Normal opening hours: noon–2.30pm for lunch and 7–10/11pm for dinner. In winter they may close earlier, though there is always a handful of restaurants serving snacks or main meals until later. The restaurants are listed by *sestieri* (district).

Choose a canal-side table for a truly Venetian dining experience

San Marco

Osteria agli Assassini £

An excellent selection of Italian wines and foreign beers, served alongside traditional Venetian cuisine.
Rio Terrà degli Assassini, San Marco 3695. Landing stage: San Angelo.

Osteria Leon Bianco £

Located just off a busy square, this friendly *osteria* serves good-value meals and traditional Venetian bar snacks.
Salizzada San Luca, San Marco 4153.
Tel: 340 892 0803.
Open: Mon–Sat noon–3pm & 7–10pm.
Landing stage: Rialto.

Da Raffaele ££

This restaurant in an idyllic canal-side spot has been running for more than 60 years. Fish looms large on the menu and is great value in this expensive part of town.
Ponte delle Ostreghe, San Marco 1322.
Tel: 041 523 2317. www. ristorantedaraffaele.com.
Open: Fri–Wed noon–3pm & 7–10.30pm.
Landing stage: Santa Maria del Giglio.

Osteria San Marco ££–£££

This compact eatery has deservedly made a name for itself, with a small but perfectly honed menu and a superb wine list.
Frezzeria, San Marco 1610. Tel: 041 528 5242.
www.osteriasanmarco.it.
Open: Mon–Sat 12.30–11pm. Landing stage: Vallaresso.

Antico Martini £££

Situated alongside La Fenice, this is the perfect location for pre- or post-theatre meals. Traditional Venetian food is served with discretion and elegance.
Campiello della Fenice, San Marco 2007.
Tel: 041 522 412.
www.anticomartini.com.
Open: noon–3pm lunch; 3–6pm light meals; 6–11.30pm dinner.
Landing stage: Sant'Angelo.

Centrale £££

A lounge-restaurant, handy for the Fenice theatre. The cuisine is a combination of Mediterranean and regional ingredients, and wine connoisseurs can choose from 800 vintages. Open evenings only, but until 2am.
Piscina Frezzeria, San Marco 1659.
Tel: 041 296 0664.
www.centrale-lounge.com.
Landing stage: San Marco.

Harry's Bar ££££

This was the haunt of Ernest Hemingway who liked the carpaccio here. Now patronised by affluent celebrity-spotters. Excellent home-made pasta – at a price.
Calle Vallaresso, San Marco 1323.
Tel: 041 528 5777.
Landing stage: San Marco.

San Polo and Santa Croce

Naranzaria £

A fashionable restaurant on the Grand Canal, with a simple menu.
Erbaria, San Polo 130.
Tel: 041 724 1035.
www.naranzaria.it.
Landing stage: Rialto.

Nono Risorto £

Trattoria with garden, serving pizzas, Venetian snacks and main meals.
Sottoportego di Sior Bettina, Santa Croce 2338. Tel: 041 524 1169.
Landing stage: San Stae.

La Zucca ££

The setting is picture-perfect and the food is fabulous. If you are tired of Venetian fare, head here for a superb range of meat and vegetarian dishes. In honour of its name, pumpkin features strongly on its autumn menu.
Ponte del Megio, Santa Croce 1762.
Tel: 041 524 1570.
www.lazucca.it. Open: Mon–Sat noon–2.30pm & 7–10.30pm. Landing stage: San Stae.

Osteria Mocenigo ££

This attractive restaurant is in a quiet part of town, but only five minutes from the Rialto. The owners are friendly and fun, and the fishy menu always good.
Salizzada San Stae, Santa Croce 1919.
Tel: 041 523 1703.
Open: Mon–Sat noon–2.30pm & 7–10pm. Landing stage: San Stae.

Da Fiore ££££

Excellent fish and intimate setting. Booking essential.
Calle del Scaleter, San Polo 2202. Tel: 041 721 308.
www.dafiore.net. Landing stage: San Stae or San Silvestro.

Dorsoduro

Mille Vini Enoteca £

A welcome new entry in this square, heaving with tourist traps and student haunts. The wines are the stars here, but the food makes an excellent accompaniment!
Campo Santa Margherita, Dorsoduro 2929.
Tel: 041 522 3436.
www.millevini.com.
Open: Mon–Sat 10am–3pm & 6pm–midnight. Landing stage: Ca' Rezzonico.

Osteria Ai 4 Feri £

Just off Campo San Barnaba, this rough-and-ready establishment has a great selection of fishy fare. Service is quick and no-nonsense – the friendly staff will guide you through the menu.
Calle Lunga San Barnaba, Dorsoduro 2754.
Tel: 041 520 6978. Open: Mon–Sat noon–3pm & 7–10.30pm. Landing stage: Ca' Rezzonico.

Osteria-Enoteca San Barnaba ££

It's all about meat on this menu. Husband-and-wife team works wonders as sommelier and head chef respectively in this excellent restaurant.
Calle Lunga San Barnaba, Dorsoduro 2736.
Tel: 041 521 2754.
Open: noon–2.30pm & 7–10pm. Closed Wed & Thur lunch. Landing stage: Ca' Rezzonico.

L'Avogaria £££

Down a tiny alleyway near the Zattere, this atmospheric modern eatery is run by southern Italians, who also rent three charming rooms above the establishment.
Calle dell'Avogaria, Dorsoduro 1629.
Tel: 041 296 0491. www.avogaria.com. Landing stage: San Basilio.

L'Incontro £££

Informal and good value for your money. The meat is truly excellent.
Rio Terrà Canal, Dorsoduro 3062. Tel: 041 522 2404. Landing stage: Ca' Rezzonico.

Riviera £££

Open mainly for lunch. Excellent pasta, good for fish too. Nice setting by the Giudecca Canal.
Zattere, Dorsoduro 1473.
Tel: 041 522 7621.
www.ristoranteriviera.it. Landing stage: San Basilio.

Agli Alboretti £££–££££

Creative cooking of Venetian stalwarts such as risotto and fish. The walled courtyard is a leafy haven in summer.
Dorsoduro 882, Rio Terrà Foscarini. Tel: 041 523 0058. www.aglialboretti. com. Open: Thur eve–Tue noon–2.30pm & 7–10pm. Landing stage: Accademia.

Castello

Aciugheta £

Meals are served in a light modern setting.
Campo Santi Filippo e Giacomo, Castello 4357. Tel: 041 522 4292. Landing stage: San Zaccaria, San Marco.

Dai Tosi £

Make sure you go to the right place as there are two eateries bearing the same name in this street. Popular with locals and ideal after traipsing around the Biennale, it's worth booking ahead.
Seco Marina, Castello 738. Tel: 041 523 7102. Open: Mon–Tue & Thur noon–2pm, Fri–Sun noon–2pm & 7–10pm. Landing stage: Giardini or Giardini Biennale.

Alle Testiere ££

Well-known small venue specialising in fish.
Calle del Mondo Novo, Castello 5801. Tel: 041 522 7220. Landing stage: Rialto.

Ristorante Al Covo £££–££££

American-Venetian owners Diane and Cesare serve up mouthwatering dishes. No prizes for guessing that fish features predominantly on the menu, but it's all delicious. Diane's desserts are deservedly renowned.
Campiello della Pescaria, Castello 3968. Tel: 041 522 3812. www. ristorantealcovo.com. Open: Fri–Tue noon–2.30pm & 7–10pm. Landing stage: Arsenale.

Corte Sconta ££££

Unpretentious restaurant, serving some of the best fish in the city.
Calle del Pestrin, Castello 3886. Tel: 041 522 7024. Landing stage: Arsenale.

Cannaregio

Osteria Antica Adelaide £

Though service is on the slow side, savour your wine while awaiting the Venetian specialities. What makes chef-owner Alvise Ceccato stand out is that a percentage of proceeds goes to charity.
Calle Priuli Racheta, Cannaregio 3728. Tel: 041 523 2629. Open: daily noon–2.30pm & 6.30–10pm. Landing stage: Ca' d'Oro.

Osteria l'Orto dei Mori ££

This little gem of a restaurant has outdoor seating in summer, with the Mori statues eyeing up your dinner. Serving up a more unusual menu than most, the warm salad of artichokes and prawns is a must.
Campo dei Mori, Cannaregio 3386. Tel: 041 524 3677. www.osteria ortodeimori.com. Open: Wed–Mon noon–2.30pm & 7–10pm. Landing stage: Madonna dell'Orto.

Vini da Gigio £££

Classy fish restaurant with an old-fashioned feel. Great wines and good service.
Fondamenta della Chiesa, Cannaregio 3628A. Tel: 041 528 5140. www. vinidagigio.com. Landing stage: Ca' d'Oro.

WINES AND WINE BARS

Northeast Italy produces an extensive variety of wines, many of them from the Veneto. The most familiar names are the red Valpolicella and Bardolino, and the white Soave.

However, most of the house wine served in restaurants in Venice comes from the Friuli region to the north of the city. These very palatable wines include Merlot, Pinot Nero and Cabernet (reds), and Pinot Grigio, Tocai and Sauvignon (whites).

Prosecco, a light sparkling white wine from Conegliano in the Veneto, makes an ideal aperitif. It is very popular with Venetians and is to be found in nearly all bars and restaurants. The local firewater is *grappa*. Bassano del Grappa in the Veneto has been the centre of the Grappa region since the 18th century.

The most authentic venue in which to try Italian wines is a *bacaro*, an old Venetian wine bar with little or no seating, but plenty of local atmosphere. They can be found all over Venice, most of them serving Venetian snacks to go with the wines.

The following glossary and list of places specialising in wines will help you drink (and eat) your way around the city, Venetian style.

Ombra: a glass of wine, so called because of the old tradition of purchasing a glass of wine at stalls which used to stand in the shade (*ombra*) of the Campanile in Piazza San Marco.

A cargo of wine makes its way along the canals of Venice

Spritz: a Venetian aperitif of white wine, sparkling water and a dash of Select, Bitter or Aperol.

Bellini: the speciality of Harry's Bar, concocted by Arrigo Cipriani. It is normally made up of Prosecco and peach juice.

Cicheti: snacks such as baby fried squid, meat balls, artichoke hearts, pieces of cheese or ham, often served with wine.

Wine bars

Al Portego

A popular haunt for students, this bar-cum-trattoria has a wide range of bar snacks, wines and beers and reasonable prices. Though not the prettiest spot in town, it's certainly one of the liveliest come *aperitivo* time.

San Lio, Castello 6015. Tel: 041 522 9038. Open: 10.30am–2.30pm & 5.30–10pm. Landing stage: Rialto.

Bar Marcà

Tiny welcoming bar with tasty snacks, right in the market.

Erberia Rialto, San Polo 213. Landing stage: Rialto.

Cantine del Vino già Schiavi

Good choice of wines to taste and bottles on sale to take away. Directly across from the famous gondola boatyard. Standing room only.

Fondamenta Nani 992, Dorsoduro. Landing stage: Accademia.

Do Mori

The quintessential *bacaro*, serving excellent wines and *cicheti*. Always packed with locals. Standing room only.

Calle do Mori (off Ruga Vecchia San Giovanni), San Polo 429. Landing stage: Rialto.

La Cantina

Delectable snacks and connoisseur wines.

Strada Nova, Cannaregio 3689. Landing stage: Ca' d'Oro.

Osteria al Milion

Old wine bar located in a small square near Marco Polo's family house. Serves snacks and main meals, including Venetian specialities such as *pasta e fagioli* and *fegato alla veneziana*.

Corte al Milion, Cannaregio 5841. Landing stage: Rialto.

Trattoria All'Arco

Though neither as quaint nor as expensive as its neighbour, Do Mori, nevertheless this eatery is a strong contender for San Polo's top position in the *cicheti* and wine stakes.

Ruga dei Due Mori, San Polo 436. Tel: 041 520 5666. Open: Mon–Sat 8.30am–8pm. Landing stage: Rialto Mercato or San Silvestro.

Un Mondo diVino

Elbow your way into this great favourite with *cicheti* eaters, which serves a mouthwatering array of tasty bar snacks. The wine list is also large, unlike the venue, a one-time butcher's shop.

Salizada San Canciano, Cannaregio 5984A. Tel: 041 521 1093. Open: Tue–Sun 10am–3pm & 5.30–9.30pm. Landing stage: Rialto.

Vino Vino

Wine bar near the Fenice; also serves meals and snacks.

Ponte delle Veste, San Marco 2007a. Landing stage: Santa Maria del Giglio or San Marco.

Accommodation

Venice has hundreds of hotels, from basic 1-star establishments in back alleys to splendid palaces overlooking the lagoon or Grand Canal. Whatever the category, you can count on paying up to 30 per cent more than for the equivalent hotel on the mainland. Offset against this is the pleasure of waking up to church bells and chugging barges rather than a klaxon or roaring Vespa.

Hotels are graded from 1-star to 5-star luxury, and there are also bed-and-breakfast establishments with costs varying considerably. The Venice Tourist Board and the Venice Hoteliers' Association produces an annual list of hotels of all categories, detailing their facilities and prices.

For many months of the year you will need to book your accommodation well in advance. The most crowded times are from June to the end of September, at Christmas and at Carnevale time in February.

Midsummer is not necessarily more of a problem than late spring or early autumn, since a large proportion of visitors at this time are merely day-trippers. January is the quietest month, and some of the hotels close down completely.

The Lido is strictly seasonal and most hotels are closed between November and April.

In some hotels you can specify a room with a view, for which you pay a supplement; at other hotels it is just a case of pot luck.

Few hotels have their own restaurant, which is no disadvantage given that the city is so liberally endowed with places to eat. Many do serve breakfast, but this cuts out entirely the rather more pleasant option of breakfasting at a bar or café where the coffee and croissants are cheaper – and usually superior, besides – than what is offered in a hotel.

If you are going to Venice independently of a tour operator or travel agent, you should email, telephone or fax a hotel in advance unless booking online. This can be done in English, even to the smallest hotel.

You are normally asked for a deposit equivalent to the cost of one night's stay, which can be paid through a credit card. Failure to turn up or to inform the hotel in advance of cancellation will normally incur the loss of this deposit.

Those who arrive in Venice on spec can contact the Hotel Information offices at the airport (*Tel: 041 541*

5133), the station (*Tel: 041 715 288*), Piazzale Roma (*Tel: 041 522 8640*), the Tronchetto parking lot (*Tel: 041 528 7833*) and the Rotonda Autostradale Villabona Sud (Marghera Autostrada) (*Tel: 041 921 638*), or else you can call the Last Minute booking service (freephone number in Italy: *800 84 3006; 39 041 522 2264 from abroad*); or contact *www.veniceinfo.it*

CAMPING AND HOSTELS

Rolling Venice (*see p187*) produces an excellent leaflet on cheap accommodation in Venice. Aimed at young people, this consists of basic rooms or dormitory accommodation in hostels and religious institutions.

Tourist offices also offer information on cheap accommodation in Venice.

Camping Alba d'Oro

This campsite boasts its own pool, plus shops and eateries. It's easy to reach from the airport and is only a 20-minute bus ride into Venice.
Via Triestina 214/G, Ca' Noghera. Tel: 041 541 5102. www.camping.it/veneto/albadoro/

Camping Fusina

Just across the causeway from Venice, this is great for caravanners and campers, though mobile homes can also be rented. It's a short bus ride from the city.
Via Moranzani, Fusina. Tel: 041 547 0055. www.camping-fusina.com

Foresteria Valdese

This lovely palace offers a variety of options for budget travellers, from a bed in a dorm to double rooms overlooking a canal. A great spot from which you can reach most sights on foot.
Calle Lunga Santa Maria Formosa Castello 5170. Tel: 041 528 6797. www.foresteriavenezia.it

IYH Ostello Venezia

One of the first and still the best of the hostels on offer. Clean rooms in a lovely setting overlooking the Zattere, this is a great spot for budget travellers. YHA membership required.
Giudecca 86, Fondamenta Zitelle. Tel: 041 523 8211. www.ostellovenezia.it

Many Venetian hotels are converted from former palaces

HOTELS

Price for two people in a double room, with breakfast:

£	less than €110
££	€110–200
£££	€200–320
££££	over €320

San Marco

Ca' Miani £

A stone's throw from Campo Santo Stefano, with the Accademia Bridge and Palazzo Grassi literally around the corner, this stylish B&B places you in the heart of the city.

Calle del Frutarol, San Marco 2865.
Tel: 041 241 1868.

Hotel Novecento £–££

This charming boutique hotel is just a short walk from Saint Mark's Square. The décor has an ethnic feel, with dark woods and bright fabrics.

Calle del Dose, San Marco 2683/4. Tel: 041 241 3765.
www.novecento.biz

Westin Europa & Regina £££

Great location and lovely terrace restaurant on the Grand Canal.

Calle Larga 22 Marzo, San Marco 2159.
Tel: 041 240 0001.
www.westin.com

Starhotel Splendid £££–££££

Ideally situated in the heart of the San Marco area, just a short walk to the major sights. Watch gondolas gliding past as you breakfast in the hotel restaurant.

Mercerie, San Marco 760.
Tel: 041 520 0755.
www.starhotels.com/hotel/splendid_venice

The Gritti Palace has a prime location on the Grand Canal

Gritti Palace ££££
Once home to a doge, this is Venetian old-style elegance at its best.
Campo Santa Maria del Giglio, San Marco 2467. Tel: 041 794 611. www. starwood.com/grittipalace

San Polo and Santa Croce
Al Gallion £–££
This pristine B&B is run by the delightful Daniela and provides double and family rooms. Easy to reach from both the train and the bus station, it's a great starting point for a short break.
Calle Gallion, Santa Croce 1126. Tel: 041 524 4743. www.algallion.com

Al Ponte Mocenigo £–££
One of the best of the many boutique hotels that have sprung up in the city over recent years. Situated on a pretty canal, it combines typical Venetian interiors with modern touches.
Fondamenta Rimpeto Mocenigo, Santa Croce 2063. Tel: 041 524 4797. www.alpontemocenigo.com

Oltre Il Giardino ££
A great location in the centre of the city, this pretty hotel has just six rooms and a cosy feel. Start the day with breakfast in the walled garden.
Fondamenta Contarini, San Polo 2542. Tel: 041 275 0015. www. oltreilgiardino-venezia.com

Ca' Nigra Lagoon Resort £££
A stately palace on the Grand Canal, this hotel is situated in a quiet and pretty *campo* not far from the Frari. Each bathroom comes equipped with a whirlpool and there are two gardens for relaxing in.
Campo San Simeon Grande, Santa Croce 927. Tel: 041 275 0047. www.hotelcanigra.it

Hotel Palazzo Giovanelli £££
After decades of standing forlorn, the Palazzo finally reopened as this attractive 4-star hotel. The location is ideal: close to a *vaporetto* stop, Rialto Bridge a mere five minutes' walk away and sweeping views of the Grand Canal to boot.
Calle Pesaro, Santa Croce 2070. Tel: 041 525 6040. *www.hotelpalazzo giovanelli.com*

Dorsoduro
Avogaria £
Though primarily a restaurant, Avogaria has three attractive rooms, including the junior suite with a private courtyard. Added touches in the other rooms include showers for two.
Calle dell'Avogaria, Dorsoduro 1629. Tel: 041 296 0491. www.avogaria.com

Ca' della Corte £–££
This immaculate bed and breakfast is ideal for those arriving by road. Apartments are also available for groups or families.
Corte Surian, Dorsoduro 3560. Tel: 041 715 877. www.cadellacorte.com

Locanda Ca' Zose £–££
A pretty little hotel on a charming canal, it is run by two sisters. Close to all the modern and contemporary art spaces and just steps away from the Accademia.
Calle del Bastion Dorsoduro 193/B. Tel: 041 522 6635. www.hotelcazose.com

Ca' Pisani £££–££££

Located just behind the Accademia Galleries, this 15th-century palace is all about mod cons and 1940s glamour. Service is excellent and the hotel restaurants exemplary.
Rio Terrà Foscarini, Dorsoduro 979A. Tel: 041 240 1411. www.capisanihotel.it

Ca' Maria Adele ££££

One of the swishest hotels in town, this bijou establishment is situated next to the Salute Church and the Punta della Dogana. The interiors are sumptuous and the surroundings divine.
Rio Terrà dei Catecumeni, Dorsoduro 111. Tel: 041 520 3078. www.camariaadele.it

Cannaregio

B&B Alla Fraterna £

In the shopping district of town and close to the Rialto Bridge, this is a bargain B&B. Friendly owners Stefano and Mikela will help you enjoy your stay.
Rio Terrà del Bagatin, Cannaregio 5922. Tel: 041 520 3061.

Boscolo Hotel dei Dogi £££

Tucked away far from the madding crowds, this hotel boasts a garden overlooking the northern lagoon. After a hard day's sightseeing, relax in the splendid spa.
Fondamenta Madonna dell'Orto, Cannaregio 3500. Tel: 041 220 8111. www.boscolohotels.com

Castello

Metropole £££

If it is old-style luxury you are after, then the Metropole is for you. With lavish suites overlooking the lagoon and the only restaurant in town with two Michelin stars, the hotel offers old-fashioned sophistication.
Riva degli Schiavoni, Castello 4149. Tel: 041 520 5044. www.hotelmetropole.com

Danieli ££££

Though looking a little shabbier than the new upstart hotels in town, the Danieli remains a bastion of Venetian hotelery.
Riva degli Schiavoni, Castello 4196.

Tel: 041 522 6480. www.danielihotelvenice.com

Venice environs

Bauer Palladio Hotel £££

A new addition to the handful of fabulous hotels on the Giudecca, the Palladio has views of Saint Mark's basin. The tastefully decorated rooms are a haven of tranquillity.
Fondamenta San Giovanni, Giudecca 33. Tel: 041 270 3806. www.bauerhotels.com

Hotel Excelsior ££££

Glamour is at the core of this hotel. During the Film Festival, it is positively teeming with stars and wannabes.
Lungomare Marconi, 41, Venice Lido. Tel: 041 526 0201. www.hotelexcelsiorvenezia.com

Hotel Molino Stucky ££££

The new Hilton Molino Stucky boasts a rooftop pool and glamorous skyline bar, not to mention a gorgeous spa.
Giudecca, 810. Tel: 041 272 3311. www.hilton.com

San Clemente Palace ££££

The elite San Clemente Palace is a hotel complex on its own island, 15 minutes by shuttle launch from Piazza San Marco. It boasts tennis courts and a pool.
Isola di San Clemente. Tel: 041 244 5111. www.sanclemente.thi.it

SELF-CATERING

Self-catering accommodation in Venice is plentiful, and given the high cost of hotels and eating out, it is worth considering for a family staying in the city for a week or more.

Venetian Apartments

This London-based company has a long history of renting in Venice. All types and sizes available, as well as helpful staff to help accommodate you.
271 Regent St, London, UK. Tel: (0044) 203 178 4180. www.venice-rentals.com

Venice Holidays

A wide choice of rental options include ground-floor apartments with gardens on the Grand Canal. The English-speaking agents will make sure you have everything you need.
Calle dei Fuseri, San Marco 4456. Tel: 041 260 2334/328 248 9102. www.venice-holidays.com

Venice Rentals

This lovely husband-and-wife team have a good selection of quality apartments and houses in Venice and on the Lido. One of the most reliable self-catering companies in the city.
90 Sea St, Suite 121, Weymouth MA, USA. Tel: (001) 617 472 5392. www.veniceitaly apartments.com

The Hilton Molino Stucky, a new luxury hotel, opened in 2007

Practical guide

Arriving

Passports and visas

Visitors from EU countries, the USA, Canada, Australia and New Zealand can stay for up to three months with a passport only, but it must be valid for at least five months.

By air

Marco Polo airport is located on the mainland at Tessera, 9km (5¹/2 miles) north of Venice. The most spectacular entrance to the city is by water. The journey by public launch to San Marco, via the Lido, takes the best part of an hour. The alternative is a private water-taxi which costs seven times as much (be sure to settle the price before boarding). The cheapest form of transport is a bus from the airport to Piazzale Roma, Venice's road traffic terminus. The ATVO buses run regularly, though the half-hourly (every 15 mins at peak times) public ACTV bus (No 5) is cheaper.

Treviso airport, 30km (18¹/2 miles) north of Venice, is used by many charter flights. Coaches are organised for transport to Venice.

By rail

A train service is available from London via Paris to Venice. The most luxurious form of travel is the Venice Simplon Orient Express from London to Venice, which runs weekly, and occasionally twice-weekly, from the end of March to the beginning of November. For more information, contact them on *0845 077 2222. www.orient-express.com*

The Thomas Cook European Timetable includes up-to-date information on rail services to Italy and can be purchased in the UK from any branch of Thomas Cook, at some railway stations and bookshops, call *(01733) 416477* or visit *www.thomascookpublishing.com*

The arrival point for trains in Venice is Venezia–Santa Lucia (not the mainland station, Venezia–Mestre), which has a tourist office, a bank, left-luggage facilities, a porter service and a wide choice of water transport.

By road

The queues on the causeway in summer and the high price of parking are good reasons for not taking your car to Venice. The choices of car parks are Piazzale Roma, where space is at a premium, and Tronchetto, an island linked to the city by a bridge. Both are well served by waterbuses to central

Waterbuses are a cheap way of getting around

Venice, and provide bureau de change and tourist information services. The car parks on the mainland at San Giuliano in Mestre and at Fusina are cheaper. Both are connected to Venice by bus and waterbuses.

Camping

There are no campsites in Venice itself. On the mainland there are sites at Fusina, Mestre and Marghera (*see Accommodation p173*). More desirable (and more expensive) are the sites along the Litorale del Cavallino, between Jesolo and Punta Sabbioni, which is linked to Venice by ferry.

Children

Children under four years of age travel free on waterbuses. Most restaurants welcome children. Hotels can normally organise a babysitter. Disposable nappies and baby food are available from pharmacies, but are cheaper from supermarkets. (*See also pp160–61.*)

Climate

The weather is at its most pleasant in spring and autumn. July and August are uncomfortably hot. Winters can be cold (average temperature 4°C/39°F) and the city is sometimes flooded.

Conferences and congresses

Zitelle Cultural Centre for Exhibitions and Communication Located on the island of Giudecca, the centre is focused around the restored Church of the Zitelle. The exhibition area is divided into 17 halls, plus conference rooms for 20–70 people. Services include interpreters for simultaneous and consecutive translations, secretarial assistance and multilingual hostesses. *Giudecca 34, 30133 Venice. Tel: 041 270 4111. www.zitelle.it. Vaporetto: Nos 2 & 41/42 run every 10 minutes from San Marco. Alternatively, take a water-taxi.*

Centro Congressi di Venezia On the Venice Lido, this extensive centre caters for 20 to 1,500 participants and offers a full range of conference services. Access is by *vaporetto* or bus from the main landing stages for ferries from Venice. The Lido's Nicelli airfield for light planes is an added bonus. *Lungomare Marconi 30, Lido. Tel: 041 242 0330. www.veniceconvention.com*

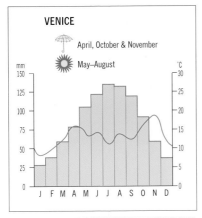

WEATHER CONVERSION CHART

25.4mm = 1 inch
°F = 1.8 × °C + 32

Crime

Venice is the safest large city in Italy and you can wander the streets at night without any threat. However, there is occasional petty crime, mostly pick-pockets, so keep an eye on valuables, especially in crowds and on waterbuses. In the event of theft, obtain a police report in order to claim for insurance.

Driving

Though Venice is connected to the mainland by road bridge, no road communications exist within the city itself. Drivers have to leave their vehicles in multistorey garages or open-air car parks outside the city. Parking is limited, especially in summer. Car parks at Piazzale Roma are the most convenient, with a *vaporetto* landing stage and taxi-stand. The municipal car park (Autorimessa Comunale di Venezia) at the end of the bridge has the most reasonable prices. There is parking at ever-expanding Tronchetto, with good *vaporetto* services to the centre of Venice. Car parking charges vary, depending on the time of year, length of stay and size of vehicle, but it is never cheap. You could leave your vehicle on the mainland, but avoid roadside parking as break-ins are common.

Breakdown

In the event of a breakdown, call *803 116*, the number for the Automobile Club d'Italia (ACI). All foreign motorists driving cars with foreign plates will be assisted free of charge. Use this number even if you have an accident: the ACI will help with police formalities and the exchange of insurance details.

Documents

If you hold an old green UK licence, you must obtain and carry an official translation (available from AA offices). No translation is necessary if you hold a pink European licence. If you are driving your own car in Italy, you will need to carry the registration and MOT documents and an international green insurance card (not necessary for cars with British plates). If you are hiring a car in Italy, the rental company will supply these.

Petrol

Petrol stations are usually open Monday to Friday, 7.30am–noon and 4–7pm, and the majority of them, except *autostrada* service stations, close on Saturday, Sunday and public holidays. Many petrol stations accept credit cards. Two types of petrol are sold: *Super* (4-star) and *Super senza piombo* (unleaded). Diesel is sold as *gasolio*.

Rental
Hertz Rent A Car
Piazzale Roma 496/A. Tel: 041 528 4091. www.hertz.com.
Marco Polo Airport. Tel: 041 541 6075.
Avis
Piazzale Roma, 496/G.
Tel: 041 523 7377. www.avis.com.
Marco Polo Airport. Tel: 041 541 5030.

Rules of the road

Traffic drives on the right. Speed limits are 50km/h (31mph) in built-up areas, 90km/h (56mph) on secondary roads, 110km/h (68mph) on *superstrade* and 130km/h (81mph) on *autostrade*. Seat belts must be worn and children under 12 must sit in the rear. Using the horn is prohibited in built-up areas except in emergencies; flash your lights instead. Strict laws limit a driver's permissable blood-alcohol level to 0.08 per cent, and those driving while using a mobile phone will be fined.

Electricity

The voltage is 220 volts AC and most sockets take the round two-pin adaptor plugs.

Embassies and consulates

UK (consulate) *Piazza Donatori Sangue 2, Mestre. Tel: 041 505 5990.*
Australia (embassy) *Via Antonio Bosio 5, Rome. Tel: 06 852721.*
Canada (embassy) *Via Zara 30, Rome. Tel: 06 854442911.*
USA (embassy) *Via Vittorio Veneto 121, Rome. Tel: 06 852541.*

Emergency telephone numbers

General *113*
Carabinieri (Police) *112*
Fire *115*
Ambulance *118*
The **Ospedale Civile** (Civil Hospital), Campo Santi Giovanni e Paolo (*Tel: 041 529 4111*), has a 24-hour casualty department.

Health

No vaccinations are needed for a visit to Italy. All EU countries have reciprocal arrangements for reclaiming medical expenses. UK residents should obtain the European Health Insurance Card (EHIC) from any UK post office.

To cover all eventualities a travel insurance policy is advisable, and for non-EU residents, essential.

Chief everyday health hazards are: too much sun, air pollution in large cities (not Venice itself) and biting insects.

Maps

A wealth of accurate detailed city maps is available at tourist offices, bookshops and souvenir stands. For finding addresses that give no more than the *sestiere* (or quarter) and its number, Venetians use the *Calli, Campielli e Canali* (published by Helvetia in Italian and English, and available at the Goldoni bookshop, *Calle dei Fabbri, San Marco 4742/3*).

Media

The main Italian daily newspapers are *La Repubblica* and *Il Corriere della Sera*. The financial national daily paper is *Il Sole-24 Ore*, and the main business weekly is *Il Mondo*. The two local newspapers on sale in Venice are the *Gazzettino* and the *Nuova Venezia*, both of which provide up-to-date information and a calendar of events. A vast array of international newspapers is widely available and top-class hotels have satellite TV.

Money matters

Italy has adopted the euro (€) as of 2002. Notes come in denominations of €500, €200, €100, €50, €20, €10 and €5; coins in €2, €1, then 50, 20, 10, 5, 2 and 1 cents. Banks are concentrated in Campo San Bartolomeo and Calle Larga XXII Marzo, along with Strada Nuova. Bank opening hours are usually Monday to Friday, 8.30am– 1.30pm and 2.35–3.35pm or 3–4pm. Bureaux de change have longer opening hours.

Electronic exchange machines with multilingual instructions can be found at the airport, railway station and banks throughout the city. Credit cards can be used in many establishments, the most widely accepted being VISA and MasterCard. Automatic cash dispensers, taking VISA and MasterCard, can be found at most banks. Traveller's cheques are the safest means of carrying money, but beware of their set commission charges.

National and local holidays

Shops, offices and banks are closed on:
1 January New Year's Day
6 January Epiphany
March/April, variable Easter Monday
25 April Liberation Day
1 May Labour Day
2 June Anniversary of the Founding of the Republic
15 August Assumption Day
1 November All Saints' Day
8 December Immaculate Conception
25 December Christmas Day
26 December St Stephen's Day

CONVERSION TABLE

FROM	TO	MULTIPLY BY
Inches	Centimetres	2.54
Feet	Metres	0.3048
Yards	Metres	0.9144
Miles	Kilometres	1.6090
Acres	Hectares	0.4047
Gallons	Litres	4.5460
Ounces	Grams	28.35
Pounds	Kilograms	0.4536
Tons	Tonnes	1.0160

To convert back, divide by the number in the third column.

Opening hours

Shops are generally open Monday to Saturday, 8/9am to 1pm and 4pm to 7/8pm, though many are also open during the afternoon and on Sundays during the summer. **Churches** all have different timetables, but in general are open 7/8am–noon and 4/5–7pm. The opening hours of museums and galleries vary considerably but the tourist offices in Venice can provide a current list of them. *See also the* Destination Guide *for specific openings.*

Organised tours

Local companies organise tours around the city and islands. Organised boat trips are also worth taking – either down the Grand Canal or across to Murano, Burano and Torcello. (*See pp136–7 & 140 for trips down the Brenta Canal.*)

Information is available from any travel agency in the city, from tourist offices or from hotels.

Practical guide

Pharmacies

Italian pharmacists are well trained. Local newspapers and the booklet *Un Ospite di Venezia* list late-night pharmacies, and the week's shift is displayed on all pharmacy doors. Many pharmacists speak some English.

Places of worship

The population is predominantly Roman Catholic, and Mass is celebrated in churches on Sundays. The times are listed outside the churches.

The Basilica San Marco (*Tel: 041 522 5205*) celebrates Mass eight or nine times daily, except on Saturdays when one evening Mass is held.

The Church of San Giorgio Maggiore (*Tel: 041 522 7827*) holds Mass with Gregorian chant on Sundays at 11am.

St George's Anglican Church (*Dorsoduro 870. Tel: 041 520 0571*) holds Sunday Matins at 10.30am and Communion at 11.30am.

The Jewish Synagogue (*Ghetto Vecchio, Cannaregio. Tel: 041 715 359*) holds services on Saturdays at 9.30am.

Post offices

The main post office is at San Marco 6016 in the Merceria, near the Rialto Bridge, and is open Monday to Friday from 8.30am to 6pm and Saturday 8.30am to 1.30pm. Telephone, telegram and fax services are available. The most central branch office is in Calle Larga dell'Ascensione, just west of Piazza San Marco, open Monday to Friday from 8.30am to 1.30pm.

Public transport

See pp24–5.

Addresses

Buildings are numbered by the administrative district or *sestiere* rather than by street. A typical address such as San Marco 2604 is almost impossible for a visitor to find unaided. If you are taking note of an address, be sure to ask for a landmark or the name of the street.

Gondolas

Consult the booklet *Un Ospite di Venezia* for the official rates. The minimum time of hire is 50 minutes. Prices rise after 8pm.

(*Cont. on p186*)

Worship in the glorious Basilica San Marco

Language

Many Venetians speak at least some English, but any attempt at Italian is always appreciated. Words generally sound as they are written. The following are the main exceptions:

c before e or i is soft, pronounced ch, so centro is pronounced chen'troh

g is also soft before e or i, so giro is pronounced jee'roh

ch or gh are both hard, so chiesa sounds like keeay'zah and ghetto like get'toh

sc before e or ie sounds like sh, so scena is pronounced shay'nah.

h is not sounded

z is pronounced ts

gli is pronounced lee

gn sounds like ny, so signora is pronounced seen-yoh'rah.

USEFUL VOCABULARY

ca' (casa)	palace or grand mansion
calle	alleyway, narrow street
campanile	bell tower
campo	a square or wide-open space
fondamenta	street running alongside a canal
ramo	alleyway between two streets
rio	small canal
rio terrà (terà)	filled-in canal
riva	a wide *fondamenta*
ruga	street lined with shops
palazzo	palace
piscina	a filled-in pond forming a street or square
salizzada	main street (formerly a paved street)
sandolo	flat-bottomed skiff
sestiere	district of Venice
sottoportego	passage or alley under private buildings
traghetto	ferry gondola across the Grand Canal

MONTHS OF THE YEAR

January	Gennaio
February	Febbraio
March	Marzo
April	Aprile
May	Maggio
June	Giugno
July	Luglio
August	Agosto
September	Settembre
October	Ottobre
November	Novembre
December	Dicembre

DAYS OF THE WEEK

Sunday	Domenica
Monday	Lunedì
Tuesday	Martedì
Wednesday	Mercoledì
Thursday	Giovedì
Friday	Venerdì
Saturday	Sabato

BASIC ITALIAN WORDS AND PHRASES

yes	sì
no	no
please	per favore
thank you	grazie
hello or goodbye	ciao (informal)
good morning	buon giorno
good afternoon/ evening	buona sera
goodnight	buona notte
excuse me	scusi
that's all right	va bene
you're welcome	prego
Do you speak English?	Parla inglese?
I do not understand	non ho capito
how much/many?	quanto/quanti?
where is?	dov'è?
I don't speak Italian	Non parlo italiano
Open/Closed	Aperto/chiuso
Entrance/Exit	Entrata/uscita
Reservation/ booking	Una prenotazione
Breakfast	Colazione
Lunch	Pranzo
Dinner	Cena
The bill	Il conto
A single/twin/ double room	Una camera singola/ doppia/matrimoniale

NUMBERS

one	uno
two	due
three	tre
four	quattro
five	cinque
six	sei
seven	sette
eight	otto
nine	nove
ten	dieci

TRANSPORT

Bus	Autobus
Coach	Pullman
Train	Treno
Railway	La ferrovia
Platform	Binario
Ticket/s	Biglietto/i
One way	Solo andata
Return	Andata e ritorno
Right	Destra
Left	Sinistra

COMMUNICATIONS

Phone	Telefono
Email	Posta elettronica
Fax	Fax
Stamp/s	Froncobollo/i
Letter	Lettera
Postcard	Cartolina
Post office	Ufficio postale

SHOPS

Bakery	Panificio
Bank	Banca
Bookshop	Libreria
Butcher's	Macelleria
Cake shop	Pasticceria
Chemist's	farmacia
Delicatessen	Salumeria
Hairdresser	Parrucchiere
Ice-cream parlour	Gelateria
Market	Mercato
Supermarket	Supermercato
Tobacconist	tabaccaio

SIGHTSEEING

Art gallery	Pinacoteca
Church	Chiesa
Garden	Giardino
Library	Biblioteca
Museum	Museo
Tourist information	Ufficio turistico

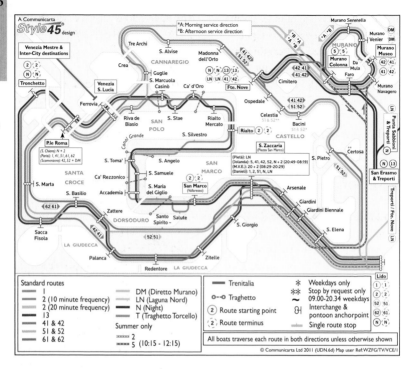

There are 12 gondola ranks, including San Marco (*Tel: 041 520 0685*), the station (*Tel: 041 718 543*) and Piazzale Roma (*Tel: 041 522 1151*). Their official website is *www.gondolieri.it*

Porters

There are eight porter ranks in the city, including San Marco (*Tel: 041 523 2385*), the station (*Tel: 041 715 272*), Piazzale Roma (*Tel: 041 522 3590*) and Accademia (*Tel: 041 522 4891*). The rates are high (starting at €15 for one piece, within the city), particularly if a porter takes your luggage on a waterbus.

Waterbuses

The waterbuses, or *vaporetti*, provide a regular and scenic service down the Grand Canal, the Canale di Cannaregio, around the periphery of Venice and to the outlying islands. Establish the correct number of your route and landing stage (most stops have two).

Tickets should be bought from ticket vendors on the landing stage (though many have closed), or from shops displaying the ACTV sign. Timed tickets (12, 24, 36, 48 and 72 hours) are good deals. Passengers travelling without a ticket will be fined.

The following are the waterbuses frequently used by tourists. The main services run every ten minutes during the day and early evening; at night services are reduced, but continuous. For further information, telephone *041 2424* or visit *www.hellovenezia.it* – or get a timetable locally.

No 1 Goes from Piazzale Roma and the station to San Marco via the Grand Canal, and on to the Lido. The boat calls at every stop along the Grand Canal.

No 2 Faster service than the No 1, going from San Marco along the Grand Canal to Tronchetto, Zattere, Giudecca, San Giorgio and San Zaccaria. In summer the route goes out to the Lido.

Nos 41/42 This scenic circular route skirts the periphery of Venice and takes in the islands of San Michele, Murano and the Lido (*see pp126–7*).

No LN The *circolare laguna nord* links the main islands in the northern lagoon (Murano, Mazzorbo, Burano and Torcello). It departs from Fondamente Nuove, otherwise from San Zaccaria to Burano via the Lido, Punta Sabbioni and Treporti. A separate link T connects with Torcello, from Burano. A special *laguna nord* ticket entitles you to unlimited travel for 12 hours on this route.

Water-taxis
There are 16 water-taxi ranks in the city, including the station, Piazzale Roma, the airport and San Marco. Prices are very high and there are extra charges. To call a water-taxi, telephone *041 723 112* or *041 522 2303*.

Senior citizens
The state museums (such as the Accademia Galleries, Ca' d'Oro and the Archaeological Museum) are free of charge for those over 65, but this applies only to citizens of the EU.

Sustainable tourism
Thomas Cook is a strong advocate of ethical and fairly traded tourism and believes that the travel experience should be as good for the places visited as it is for the people who visit them. That's why we firmly support The Travel Foundation, a charity that develops solutions to help improve and protect holiday destinations, their environment, traditions and culture. To find out what you can do to make a positive difference to the places you travel to and the people who live there, please visit *www.makeholidaysgreener.org.uk*

Student and youth travel
The **Rolling Venice** scheme has been set up for 14–29-year-olds visiting Venice.

A water-taxi speeds along the Grand Canal

For a small subscription fee, you are provided with useful booklets on itineraries, sightseeing and practical information, plus a map and a list of the cheapest accommodation.

The Rolling Venice pack is available from the tourist offices and *vaporetto* ticket booths at the major stops. Information is also available from the Informagiovani, *Via Garibaldi 155, Mestre. Tel: 041 534 6268*. The special ACTV Rolling Venice rover ticket, available from ACTV offices, enables you to travel on most boat services for 72 hours at a greatly reduced rate (see *www.hellovenezia.com* for details).

Telephones

Public telephones are plentiful, and the majority now take credit cards or Telecom phonecards, available from post offices, shops and bars displaying the public telephone symbol. Instructions are given in English. Coin telephones are being phased out. Long-distance calls are most easily made with a credit card. Calls made from hotels are more expensive.

Area codes:
UK *44*
Ireland *353*
USA *1*
Canada *1*
Australia *61*
New Zealand *64.*

For directory enquiries abroad, dial *4176*. International calls can be made through Telecom *170*.

The cheapest times to phone within Italy are after 6.30pm, from 1pm on Saturday and all day Sunday. To call Venice from abroad, dial *0039*, then the number, including the *041* code.

When phoning from Italy or from Venice itself, you should always use the *041* code as well.

Time

Local standard time is one hour ahead of Greenwich Mean Time. Italian Summer Time (when clocks go forward an hour) is in operation from the last weekend of March to the last weekend of October.

Tipping

Most restaurants and hotels include a service charge, but a small tip for a meal, to hotel staff or to a gondolier will be much appreciated. Taxi drivers expect about 10 per cent.

Toilets

The main public conveniences are at the Giardini ex Reali and the Albergo Diurno, both off Piazza San Marco, at Piazzale Roma, the railway station, Campo San Bartolomeo near the Rialto and by the Accademia Galleries, all of which you have to pay for. Otherwise, buy a drink in a café or bar.

Tourist offices

The most central tourist office is at Palazzetto Selva, San Marco. There are also offices at the railway station, the Lido (*Gran Viale 6*) – summer only – as well as Piazzale Roma and the airport. *Tel: 041 529 8711* for all these offices.

For information by post, write to the **Azienda di Promozione Turistica di Venezia**, *Castello 4421, 30122 Venezia.* See also their website *www.turismo venezia.it.* Another website that could be useful is *www.veniceconnected.com*

The Hoteliers' Association issues the free publication, *Un Ospite di Venezia*, giving, in Italian and English, lists of events, useful addresses and practical information. *Leo Bussola* is the informative bimonthly booklet published by the Tourist Board and comes with a top-grade glossy magazine.

Italian State Tourist Board (ENIT) offices abroad: *www.enit.it*

Take a gondola for a romantic and leisurely tour of the canals and a feel of old Venice

UK and **Ireland** *1 Princes Street, London W1R 8AY. Tel: (020) 7408 1254. Freephone 800 0048 2542 (from UK and Ireland).*

USA *630 Fifth Avenue, Suite 1565, New York, NY 10111.*
Tel: (212) 2454 822.

Canada *175 Bloor St E, Suite 907, South Tower, M4W 3R8, Toronto (Ontario). Tel: (416) 9254882.*

Australia *Level 4, 46 Market St, Sydney 2000, NSW. Tel: (02) 92621666.*

Travellers with disabilities

The canals, stepped bridges and some waterbuses present problems for people with disabilities. The *vaporetti* have access for wheelchairs, but the smaller, narrower *motoscafi* don't.

A clear map is available from tourist offices highlighting wheelchair-accessible areas. A number of bridges now have mechanised climbers: ask at the tourist offices for the (non-returnable) key. And accessible temporary walkways have now been erected around the city. All public toilets have wheelchair access.

The booklet *Tourism for All in the Veneto* is available free from the following places:

Informahandicap *Ca' Farsetti, San Marco 4136. Tel: 041 274 8144. www.comune.venezia.it (site currently in Italian only).*

Veneto Tourism Department *Palazzo Ziani, Fondamenta San Lorenzo, Castello 5050. Tel: 041 529 8711. www.turismovenezia.it*

Index

A

Accademia 74, 76–7, 80
Accademia Bridge 24, 90
accommodation 172–7
acqua alta 11, 20
addresses 186
air travel 178
Ala Napoleonica 56
apartments 177
Archaeology Museum 55
Armoury 44
Arquà Petrarca 141
Arsenale 104, 106, 127
Asolo 136
ATMs 182
Attila's Seat 134

B

banks 182
Baptistery 33–4
Barchessa Valmarana 137
Basilica di San Marco 26,
    28–9, 32–4, 183
Bassano del Grappa 136
beaches 129
Bellini, Giovanni 14, 42, 64,
    76, 78–9, 99, 111, 112,
    114, 118, 130
Biennale 15, 16, 117
boat tours
    Brenta Canal 136–7,
        140
    Venice periphery 126–7
    Grand Canal 90–3
Bon, Bartolomeo 59, 96,
    112
Brenta Canal 136–7, 140
Bridge of Sighs 44
Browning, Robert 80–81,
    136
Burano 130–31, 151
Byron, Lord 92, 148
Byzantine Art Museum
    121
Byzantine Empire 30

C

Ca' Contarini-Fasan 93
Ca' Foscari 90–91
Ca' Mocenigo 65, 92
Ca' d'Oro 92, 94, 96–7
Ca' Pesaro 91
Ca' Rezzonico 80–81, 84, 90
Campanile 50–51
Campiello Albrizzi 67
camping 173, 179
Campo dell'Arsenale 116
Campo dei Carmini 84
Campo dei Frari 52
Campo Ghetto Nuovo 100
Campo Manin 36
Campo dei Mori 101
Campo San Barnaba 83
Campo San Bartolomeo 36
Campo San Cassiano 66–7

Campo San Giacomo
    dell'Orio 66
Campo Santi Giovanni e
    Paolo 106–7, 111
Campo Santa Margherita
    84
Campo Santa Maria
    Formosa 110
Campo Santa Maria Mater
    Domini 66
Campo San Polo 60
Campo Santo Stefano 37
Campo San Tomà 52
Campo San Zaccaria 110
Canal Grande 6–7, 24, 35,
    38, 90–93
Canale di Cannaregio 100
Canaletto 81
Cannaregio 94–103
Canova, Antonio 39, 63
car rental 180
Carnevale 16, 18–19, 154–5
Carpaccio, Vittore 42, 59,
    77, 121
Casanova 44, 60
casino 156
Castelfranco Veneto 140
Castello 104–21
Cattedrale di Santa Maria
    dell'Assunta 134
children 160–61, 179
Chioggia 140–41
church opening hours 183
churches, visiting 21, 25
cinema 15, 17, 157
climate and seasons 20,
    179
Clock Tower 56
clothing sizes 180
Coducci, Mauro 14, 56,
    102, 107, 115, 118
Colleoni, Bartolomeo
    106–7
Collezione Peggy
    Guggenheim 84–5
Colli Euganei 141
concessions 187
Conegliano 141
conferences and congresses
    179
conversion tables 182
Correr Museum 38–9, 42
Costituzione Bridge 24
credit cards 151, 182
crime 180
culture 14–15

D

disabilities, travellers with
    189
Doges 46–7
Doge's Palace 42–5, 48–9
Dorsoduro 74–93
dress code 25
driving 178–9, 180–81

E

eating out *see* restaurants
economy 7
electricity 181
embassies and consulates
    181
emergency telephone
    numbers 181
entertainment 156–9
Euganean Hills 141

F

Fenice theatre 53, 158
festivals and events 16–19
flooding 11
Fondaco dei Tedeschi 92
Fondaco dei Turchi 91
Fondamenta Nuove 101,
    127
Fondazione Giorgio Cini
    128
food and drink 164–71
Forte di Sant'Andrea 147
Fortuny Museum 42
Frari *see* Santa Maria
    Gloriosa dei Frari
Frezzeria 53

G

Galleria Internationale
    d'Arte Moderna 60, 62
Galleria di Palazzo Cini
    85–6
Gallerie dell'Accademia 74,
    76–7, 80
gardens 146
Gesuati (Santa Maria del
    Rosario) 86
Gesuiti (Santa Maria
    Assunta) 97
Ghetto 97–8, 100
Giardini ex Papadopoli 146
Giardini Pubblici 117, 146
Giardini ex Reali 146
Giorgione 14, 76, 79, 140
Giotto 142
Giudecca 122–4, 126
glassmaking 138–9
Glass Museum 130
Goldoni, Carlo 67
gondola boatyards 82
gondolas and gondoliers
    24, 40–41, 157–8, 183,
    186
Grand Canal 6–7, 24, 35,
    38, 90–93
Guggenheim, Peggy 85

H

Harry's Bar 167
health 182
history 8–10, 30
hospitals 181
hostels 173
hotels 172–3, 174–7

I

Il Gobbo di Rialto 68
insurance 182
International Film Festival
    15, 17
Isola della Giudecca 122–4,
    126
Isola di San Michele 148–9

J

James, Henry 42, 64, 81, 86,
    93, 121
jazz and live music 159
Jewish Museum 98

L

La Pietà 116
La Rotonda 144
lace-making 135
Lace Museum 131
lagoon and islands 6, 20,
    122–35, 147–9
language 184–5
layout of Venice 24
Le Zitelle 124
Libreria Sansoviniana 51,
    54
Lido 128–9, 160
loggetta 54–5
Lombardo, Pietro 14, 52,
    102, 103, 107, 114
Longhena, Baldassare 14,
    80, 84, 86, 91, 109

M

Madonna dell'Orto 98–9,
    101
maps 182
Marciano Museum 32
Marghera 7
markets 151
masks 154–5
medical treatment 181, 182
Mercerie 36, 150
Mint 56
Molino Stucky 126
money 182
Monteverdi, Claudio 14, 63
motoscafi 24
Murano 129–30, 139,
    150–51
Museo Archeologico 55
Museo d'Arte Orientale 62
Museo Civico di Storia
    Naturale 64–5
Museo Correr 38–9, 42
Museo Diocesano d'Arte
    Sacra 107–8
Museo Dipinti Sacri
    Bizantini 121
Museo Ebraico 98
Museo dell'Estuario 135
Museo della Fondazione
    Querini Stampalia 109
Museo Fortuny 42

Museo del Merletto 131
Museo del Settecento Veneziano 81, 84
Museo Storico Navale 109
Museo del Vetro 130
music and theatre 158–9

N
national and local holidays 182
Natural History Museum 64–5
Naval History Museum 109
newspapers 181

O
Old Jewish Cemetery 129
opening hours 151, 166, 182
opera 158
Oriental Art Museum 64
Ospedaletto 109, 112

P
Padova (Padua) 141–2
Pala d'Oro 33
Palazzo Balbi 91
Palazzo Barbaro 93
Palazzo dei Camerlenghi 91
Palazzo Centani 67
Palazzo Cini Gallery 85–6
Palazzo Corner della Ca' Grande 93
Palazzo Corner Mocenigo 67
Palazzo Corner-Spinelli 92
Palazzo Dandolo 92
Palazzo Dario 90
Palazzo Ducale (Doge's Palace) 42–5, 48–9
Palazzo Grassi 49, 92–3
Palazzo Grimani 92
Palazzo Labia 100
Palazzo Mocenigo 65, 92
Palazzo Pisani-Gritti 93
Palazzo Soranzo 60
Palazzo Vendramin Calergi 92, 157
Palazzo Venier dei Leoni 84–5, 90
Palladio, Andrea 14, 112, 122, 125, 137, 144–5
Parco delle Rimembranze 117, 146
Parco Savorgnan 146
passports and visas 178
Peggy Guggenheim Collection 84–5
Petrarch 141
pharmacies 183
Piazza San Marco 49–51, 54–6, 150
Piazzetta 55–6
places of worship 183
police 181
politics 12–13
Ponte dell'Accademia 24, 90
Ponte dei Pugni 83

Ponte di Rialto 24, 36, 65, 68, 91
Ponte degli Scalzi 24
Ponte dei Sospiri 44
Ponte delle Tette 66
population 7
porters 186
post offices 183
Prigioni (Prisons) 44
Procuratie Vecchie and Nuove 56
public transport 24–5, 186–7
Punta della Dogana 82

R
Redentore 123–4
Regata Storica 17
restaurants 165–9
Rialto 65, 68, 151
Rialto Bridge 24, 36, 65, 68, 91
Riva degli Schiavoni 116
Riva dei Sette Martiri 117
Rolling Venice 161, 187–8

S
safety 180
St Mark 26, 50
St Mark's Basilica 26, 28–9, 32–4
St Mark's Square 49–51, 54–6
Salute see Santa Maria della Salute
Santi Apostoli 102
San Cassiano 68–9
Santa Croce see San Polo and Santa Croce
Santa Fosca 135
San Francesca della Vigna 112
San Francesco del Deserto 147
San Geremia 100
San Giacomo dell'Orio 69
San Giacomo di Rialto/San Giacometto 70
San Giobbe 102
San Giorgio dei Greci 110
San Giorgio Maggiore 125, 126, 128, 183
San Giorgio Maggiore (island) 124–5, 128
San Giovanni in Bragora 112–13
San Giovanni Crisostomo 111
San Giovanni Elemosinario 70
San Giovanni Evangelista 52
Santi Giovanni e Paolo 113–14
San Giuliano 56
San Lazzaro degli Armeni 147–8
San Lorenzo 110
San Marco 26–59
Santa Maria Assunta see Gesuiti

Santa Maria del Carmelo 84
Santa Maria dei Derelitti 112
Santi Maria e Donato 130
Santa Maria della Fava 57
Santa Maria Formosa 115
Santa Maria del Giglio 57
Santa Maria Gloriosa dei Frari 62–4
Santa Maria dei Miracoli 102–3
Santa Maria del Rosario see Gesuati
Santa Maria della Salute 86–8, 90
Santa Maria della Visitazione 86
San Moisè 57–8
San Nicolò dei Mendicoli 83
San Nicolò da Tolentino 52
San Pantalon 88
San Pietro di Castello 115, 118
San Pietro Martire 130
San Polo 70
San Polo and Santa Croce 60–73
San Rocco 70–71
San Salvador 58
San Sebastiano 88–9
San Servolo 148
San Stae 66
Santo Stefano 58–9
San Trovaso 89
San Vidal 59
San Zaccaria 118–20
Sansovino, Jacopo 14, 34, 44, 51, 54, 55, 56, 57, 96
Sant'Erasmo 148
Scala Contarini del Bovolo 36–7
Scalzi 92
Scalzi Bridge 24
Scuola Grande dei Carmini 84
Scuola Grande di San Giovanni Evangelista 52
Scuola Grande di San Marco 107
Scuola Grande di San Rocco 71–2
Scuola di San Giorgio degli Schiavoni 120–21
Scuola di San Nicolò dei Greci 121
self-catering 177
sestieri 24
shopping 150–55, 183
smoking 25
Sottomarina 141
souvenirs 155
Spinalunga 122
sport and leisure 162–3
Squero di San Trovaso 82
Stazione Marittima 126–7
student and youth travel 187–8

sustainable tourism 187
swimming 163
synagogues 97–8, 183

T
Teatro la Fenice 53, 158
telephones 188
Tiepolo, Giovanni Battista 14, 48, 57, 77, 81, 84, 86, 100, 102
time 188
Tintoretto 14, 43, 45, 48, 57, 59, 68–9, 70, 71–2, 76–7, 79, 86, 88, 99, 101, 125
tipping 188
Titian 14, 45, 58, 63, 64, 70, 76, 79, 80, 88, 97
toilets 188
Torcello 131, 134–5
Torre dell'Orologio 56
tourism 7, 13
tourist information 188–9
tours, organised 183
traghetti 24, 53
travel
    to Venice 20, 178–9
    within Venice 24–5, 186–7
traveller's cheques 182
Treviso 142–3

V
vaporetti 24
Veneto 135–45
Venice Card 21
Verona 143–4
Veronese, Paolo 14, 43, 44–5, 69, 74, 76, 79, 88–9, 112, 114
Villa Barbaro 145
Villa Foscari 137, 145
Villa Pisani 137–8
Villa Valmarana 145
Vincenza 145
Vivaldi, Antonio 116
Vogalonga 16

W
walks
    Arsenale and Biennale 116–17
    Cannaregio 100–101
    Castello 110–11
    Dorsoduro 82–3
    Piazzale to Piazza 52–3
    San Marco 36–7
    San Polo and Santa Croce 66–7
water-taxis 25, 187
waterbuses 24, 186–7
wildlife 133
wines and wine bars 170–71

Z
Zanipolo see Santi Giovanni e Paolo
Zattere 82, 126
Zecca 56

Acknowledgements

Thomas Cook Publishing wishes to thank the photographers, picture libraries and other organisations, to whom the copyright belongs, for the photographs in this book.

FRANCESCO ALLEGRETTO 32, 39, 45, 46, 47, 64, 65, 68, 69, 73, 87, 98, 103, 107, 108, 109, 129, 131, 138, 139, 156, 161, 163, 174
ANWER BATI 7, 15, 34, 41, 43, 48, 91, 106, 118, 119, 127, 153, 177, 178, 183
ARCHIVIO VICENSA E 145
LISA FIRTH 25, 51, 154, 189
DREAMSTIME 1 (Apho); 5 (Sailorr); 71 (Wjarek); 101 (Maui01); 124 (Inavanhateren)
FLICKR 17 (Ricc_HB74); 28 (Susanne Kortshagen); 54 (Kevin Tostado); 59, 136 (Patrick Denker); 99 (Sonya); 140 (Filippo Castagna); 149 (tanstaafl5813); 165 (Ami Shah); 187 (Clayton Parker)
FOTOLIA 166 (João Almeida); 170 (HON)
MARY EVANS PICTURE LIBRARY 78, 79
GILLIAN PRICE 12
NEIL SETCHFIELD 18, 31
SPECTRUM COLOUR LIBRARY 49, 132, 133, 142, 143
WIKIMEDIA 121 (Fb78); 144 (Hans A. Rosbach)

The remaining pictures are held in the AA PHOTO LIBRARY and were taken by DARIO MITIDIERI, with the exception of pages 55, 80, 96, which were taken by RICHARD NEWTON.

For CAMBRIDGE PUBLISHING MANAGEMENT LIMITED:
Project editor: Kate Taylor
Typesetter: Paul Queripel
Proofreaders: Jan McCann & Caroline Hunt
Indexer: Marie Lorimer

SEND YOUR THOUGHTS TO BOOKS@THOMASCOOK.COM

We're committed to providing the very best up-to-date information in our travel guides and constantly strive to make them as useful as they can be. You can help us to improve future editions by letting us have your feedback. If you've made a wonderful discovery on your travels that we don't already feature, if you'd like to inform us about recent changes to anything that we do include, or if you simply want to let us know your thoughts about this guidebook and how we can make it even better – we'd love to hear from you.

Send us ideas, discoveries and recommendations today and then look out for your valuable input in the next edition of this title.

Emails to the above address, or letters to the traveller guides Series Editor, Thomas Cook Publishing, PO Box 227, Coningsby Road, Peterborough PE3 8SB, UK.

Please don't forget to let us know which title your feedback refers to!